2001 SUPPLEMENT

to

CASES AND MATERIALS

on

NONPROFIT ORGANIZATIONS

By

JAMES J. FISHMAN
Professor of Law,
Pace University School of Law

STEPHEN SCHWARZ
Professor of Law,
Hastings College of the Law

SECOND EDITION

New York, New York
FOUNDATION PRESS
2001

 *TEXT IS PRINTED ON 10% POST CONSUMER RECYCLED PAPER*

PREFACE

This 2001 Supplement updates *Cases and Materials on Nonprofit Organizations* by summarizing the major developments that have occurred since publication of the Second Edition in the late Fall of 1999. It is organized to parallel the main text, with appropriate cross references to chapter headings and page numbers. An Appendix adds several new items to the Statutes, Regulations and Forms Supplement. This Supplement covers developments through June 15, 2001.

JAMES J. FISHMAN
STEPHEN SCHWARZ

July, 2001

TABLE OF CONTENTS

[This Table of Contents correlates the 2001 Supplement to the Table of Contents in the text, indicating the pages in the Supplement that contain material supplementing that covered under the listed original headings. Italics indicate new material.]

PART FOUR: OTHER LEGAL ISSUES AFFECTING
NONPROFIT ORGANIZATIONS

PART TWO

ORGANIZATION AND OPERATION OF NONPROFIT ORGANIZATIONS— THE STATE PERSPECTIVE

CHAPTER 2

FORMATION AND DISSOLUTION

D. DISSOLUTION AND DISTRIBUTION OF ASSETS

2. CHARITABLE TRUSTS: THE DOCTRINES OF CY PRES AND DEVIATION

Page 121:

After the first full paragraph, insert:

6A. Matter of Community Service Society. Community foundations are permanent funds endowed by many separate donors and organized to hold, manage and distribute funds in a specific geographical area either to causes specified by donors or to charities selected by the community foundation. There are over 500 such foundations that largely focus upon local needs in their communities. (See casebook, pp. 631-635.) Most funds within a community foundation are created pursuant to a separate gift instrument by which a donor (a) transfers assets to the foundation (or in the case of a trust the assets may be held by a bank or other corporate trustee), (b) sets forth the donor's wishes concerning the use of the assets and income of the fund, and (c) incorporates by reference the provisions of the community foundation's governing instrument. A defining element of a community foundation is the variance power, which provides donors with the opportunity to designate a specific charitable beneficiary but vests discretion in the community foundation to redirect the fund to a wholly different purpose. The variance power is thus broader than cy pres, which requires a court proceeding and substantial adherence to the donor's original purpose.

The Community Service Society (CSS), founded in 1846, is a social welfare agency. The New York Community Trust (NYCT), the nation's largest community foundation, administered six funds in which the donors named CSS as a beneficiary for all or a specified percentage of the income of the fund. For decades CSS received the specified income distributions. In 1971 the NYCT

1

exercised its variance power to terminate CSS's interests in the six funds. During this period CSS changed from a family agency to a social agency which meant that the organization would no longer provide direct assistance to its clientele but rather would operate with community groups in a "shared power" approach. The NYCT distribution committee justified its decision in part on the ground that governmental assistance programs supposedly rendered assistance to the poor by private charities obsolete. NYCT believed that CSS's decision to terminate its casework services justified converting the six funds into semi-designated funds and using their income for the improvement of health and welfare in New York City. CSS remained eligible to apply to NYCT for specific grants.

In 1995 CSS contended that NYCT arbitrarily exercised the variance power. In Application of the Community Service Society of New York, 275 A.D.2d 171, 713 N.Y.S.2d 712 (2000), the Supreme Court, Appellate Division affirmed a Surrogate's decision that the exercise of the variance power must be grounded in a change of circumstance that identifiably and negatively affected the designated charity to such a degree that it would prompt a donor or the fund to redirect it. However, the claims were time-barred by the statute of limitations. The case is on appeal, and if upheld, the decision would limit substantially the ability of New York community foundations to exercise the variance power to redirect donors's preferences in the absence of more formalized procedures.

3. DISTRIBUTION OF ASSETS TO PUBLIC BENEFIT ORGANIZATIONS

Page 132:

In Note 4, at the end of the carryover paragraph, insert:

The New York City Group of the Sierra Club ("the Group"), a local chapter of the national environmental organization, was involved in a vitriolic and long-running dispute with the national organization and the Atlantic Regional Chapter ("Chapter"), which covers New York State. The Group is not separately incorporated and cannot take legal action without consent of the Chapter's board of directors. Recent disputes between the Group and the Chapter involved policy issues and fundraising by the Group in contravention of Club rules. The Chapter suspended the entire board of the New York City Group. In Lane v. Sierra Club, 183 Misc.2d 944, 706 N.Y.S.2d 577 (2000), a New York Supreme Court justice found that while the Chapter had broad powers of suspension and regulation, it had violated its own procedures, because the Group had not receive sufficient notice and an opportunity to be heard prior to suspension of its leadership.

CHAPTER 3

OPERATION AND GOVERNANCE

C. FIDUCIARY OBLIGATIONS

3. THE DUTY OF LOYALTY

b. INTERESTED TRANSACTIONS

Page 217:

At the end of the first full paragraph, insert:

NOTE: BISHOP ESTATE CLOSING AGREEMENT

The Bishop Estate signed a closing agreement that gives the Internal Revenue Service extraordinary oversight of the Estate for five years, but the Estate retained its tax-exempt status by paying more than $9 million to settle a tax liability. The agreement, approved by a Hawaiian probate judge, was conditioned upon permanent removal of the incumbent trustees and presents a corporate governance roadmap that should disentangle the Estate from its previous difficulties.

The agreement requires a reorganized management structure which places day-to-day management in the hands of a chief executive officer who will independently carry out policy decisions of the board. In contrast to the past, the trustees will act as fiduciaries and exercise a more traditional policymaking and general oversight rule. The agreement requires trustees and senior executives to be subject to a conflict of interest policy. Business meetings must be documented in writing. The Estate will develop and implement a comprehensive educational and financial strategy, will create and follow an investment and spending policy, and will ensure that certified financial audits are prepared and filed annually with the probate court and provided to the attorney general and the general public. An independent internal auditing system will be implemented with procedures to ensure that individuals providing information to the auditor will not be subject to intimidation, and the internal auditor can be removed only for just cause by the trustees.

Political influence was at the root of the Estate's problems. The agreement attempts to break with the past by barring from employment current or former members of the legislative, judicial or executive branches of government until a period of three years has transpired following such employment. The Estate must adopt a lobbying policy that includes requirements for documenting communications with state and federal legislators, legislative offices and

3

committees on matters relating to the Estate. Documentation of any such communications will be made available to the master appointed by the probate court, the Hawaii attorney general and the Service. The Bishop Estate closing agreement is reported in 27 Exempt Org. Tax Rev. 174 (2000) and is available on the Estate's web site: <http://www.ksbe.edu>.

While the closing agreement only included the period from 1992 to 1996, the Service participated in a comprehensive settlement with state officials, the Bishop Estate and former trustees that released the former trustees from additional personal liability. The Estate's directors' and officers' liability insurance paid a total of $25 million including $14 million to the Estate as reimbursement for excessive compensation paid to the trustees. Stephen G. Greene, Insurer to Pay $25-Million to Settle Dispute in Hawaii, Chron. Phil., Oct. 5, 2000, at 42. The probate court appointed new trustees, of whom three were part-Hawaiian and two were alumni of the Kamehameha School. Then, in early 2001, the former trustees each reportedly agreed to pay the IRS $40,000 to settle tax deficiencies for intermediate sanctions under I.R.C. § 4958 (see infra Chapter 5E2) that were based on the IRS's allegation that the trustees had received unreasonable compensation. See Evelyn Brody, Troubling Lessons from the Bishop Estate Settlement for Administering the New Intermediate Sanctions Regime, 32 Exempt Org. Tax Rev. 431 (2001).

c. CORPORATE OPPORTUNITIES

Page 225:

After first full paragraph insert:

AMERICAN BAPTIST CHURCHES OF METROPOLITAN NEW YORK v. GALLOWAY

New York Supreme Court, Appellate Division, 2000.
271 A.D.2d 92, 710 N.Y.S.2d 12.

ROSENBERGER, J.P.

* * *

Plaintiff American Baptist Churches of Metropolitan New York ("ABC Metro") is a not-for-profit religious corporation whose charitable work includes operating Flemister House, an outreach program for AIDS patients, through two wholly-owned subsidiaries ("the Flemister plaintiffs"). ABC Metro had retained defendant Settlement Housing Fund ("SHF") in 1994 as a consultant to help develop an additional facility similar to Flemister House, namely the Noah House project at issue in the instant case.

Defendant T. Eric Galloway was first employed by SHF and later hired by ABC Metro in 1995 as Executive Director of the Flemister entities. One of his chief duties was to spearhead the Noah House project. When he was still employed by SHF, both Galloway and SHF Executive Director Carol Lamberg had developed contacts with Great Wall Development Corp, which owned a site that appeared suitable for Noah House. ABC Metro directed Galloway to proceed with negotiations and Galloway reached an oral agreement with Great Wall to purchase the property for $250,000.

Galloway also aided ABC Metro in obtaining all the necessary government approvals and securing financing for the Noah House project. Some funding was to come from a $5.6 million loan from New York City. Additionally, a private investor agreed to invest $1.8 million in return for the right to take advantage of ABC Metro's Federal income tax credits. Of these proceeds, $1.2 million would be available to ABC Metro for use in its charitable work. (As a developer of low-income housing, ABC Metro was entitled to Federal income tax credits, but it could not use them directly because it pays no Federal income taxes, so it planned to sell them to an investor in exchange for a partnership interest in the project.) ABC Metro also expected to receive a $144,000 developer's fee at closing.

By May 1996, the approvals and financing were in place. The closing of the loan from the City was contingent on a signed contract to purchase the property from Great Wall. According to the complaint, once Galloway had completed all the development work on ABC Metro's behalf, he embarked on a scheme to seize control of the Noah House project and cut ABC Metro out of the transaction entirely. Without telling ABC Metro or the Flemister plaintiffs, Galloway instructed ABC Metro's legal counsel to incorporate Community Lantern Corp. ("CLC"), a not-for-profit corporation, with himself and defendants Carol Lamberg and Craig Harwood as directors. Then, once again without plaintiffs' consent, Galloway instructed the law firm to substitute CLC's name for ABC Metro's on the purchase contract with Great Wall, and to tell Great Wall's counsel to delay the purchase.

On July 7, 1996, Galloway informed plaintiffs that he was resigning and that CLC was taking control of the Noah House project. Because of his prior relationship with Great Wall, he claimed, the property owner would not sell to ABC Metro against Galloway's wishes. Indeed, Great Wall did refuse to go through with the sale, not wishing to be caught in the dispute between CLC and ABC Metro. Great Wall subsequently offered to sell the property to ABC Metro for $350,000 if defendants approved, but ABC Metro could not finance the transaction at this substantially higher price.

The Noah House project never came to fruition. Without a signed contract, ABC Metro could not obtain the loan from the City. ABC Metro alleges that as a result, it lost the $144,000 development fee and the use of $1.2 million in proceeds from the transfer of the Noah House tax credits.

Plaintiffs then brought this action alleging fraud, breach of fiduciary duty, misappropriation of corporate opportunity, and tortious interference with prospective contractual relations. In addition to challenging the sufficiency of the 17 causes of action in the Amended Complaint on substantive grounds, defendants also argued that the Flemister plaintiffs had no standing because they had no interest in the Noah House project. The [lower] court agreed, and dismissed the Flemister entities from the lawsuit on this basis. With respect to ABC Metro, the [lower] court dismissed all its claims on the sole grounds that "[a]s a not-for-profit corporation, ABC Metro cannot satisfactorily allege damages, which would otherwise be based on lost profits." The court cited no legal authority for this proposition.

* * *

[T]he order below should be modified to reinstate all but two of ABC Metro's claims. The [lower] court erred in concluding that a not-for-profit corporation could never sustain compensable damages. First of all, as a matter of public policy, it would be unfair and counterproductive for a charitable organization to have no recourse against a dishonest fiduciary who thwarts the organization's endeavors and renders futile the expenditures of time and money invested in developing the project. Second, the [lower] court's ruling rests on a fundamental misunderstanding of the nature of a not-for-profit corporation. A not-for-profit corporation is not the same as a corporation that loses money. It is simply a corporation that devotes whatever proceeds it receives from its operations to charitable causes rather than disbursing the funds as dividends to shareholders and compensation to executives. Just as the goal of a for-profit corporation is to make money for its investors, the goal of a not-for-profit is to make money that can be spent on furthering its social welfare objectives. Both types of companies have suffered an injury when a fiduciary's misconduct frustrates these goals.

The foregoing analysis is supported by the New York Not-For-Profit Corporation Law, which clearly contemplates that not-for-profit corporations may receive income and even make an incidental profit. What distinguishes a not-for-profit is not whether it receives money, but what it does with the money. Not-For-Profit Corporation Law § 102(a)(5) defines a not-for-profit as a corporation which is organized "exclusively for a purpose or purposes, not for pecuniary profit or financial gain," and "no part of the assets, income or profit of which is distributable to, or enures to the benefit of, its members, directors or officers except to the extent permitted under this statute" (emphasis added). Section 508 allows a not-for-profit to earn an "incidental profit" from fees or charges, so long as such profits are "applied to the maintenance, expansion or operation of the lawful activities of the corporation," and not "divided or distributed in any manner whatsoever among the members, directors, or officers of the corporation."

Not-for-profit corporations in New York routinely bring actions seeking damages for breach of contract, breach of fiduciary duty and fraud. * * * While no New York case appears to have dealt with a not-for-profit's claim for diversion of a corporate opportunity, a number of cases from other states recognize that a not-for-profit may bring such a claim (e.g., White Gates Skeet Club v. Lightfine, 658 N.E.2d 864 [Ill.App.]; Valle v. North Jersey Automobile Club, 141 N.J.Super. 568, 359 A.2d 504 [N.J.App.], modified 74 N.J. 109, 376 A.2d 1192 [N.J.]; Lutherland, Inc. v. Dahlen, 357 Pa. 143, 53 A.2d 143 [Pa.]). By contrast, there is no case law supporting the [lower] court's contrary conclusion.

Here, ABC Metro pleaded at least two specific items of monetary damage flowing from defendants' alleged misconduct: the loss of ABC Metro's expected $144,000 development fee and the loss of the $1.2 million from the planned sale of Noah House's tax credits. Defendants dispute whether ABC Metro satisfied the conditions precedent to receiving these funds, but these are questions for the trier of fact. In addition, ABC Metro alleges that it has lost the money it expended to develop a project that never came to fruition because of defendants' interference. These allegations are sufficient to withstand a motion to dismiss.

Turning now to the merits of the individual causes of action, we conclude that the first through ninth and the eleventh through sixteenth causes of action asserted by ABC Metro should be reinstated.

Most of the claims encompass essentially the same allegations, phrased differently. The first cause of action alleges that Galloway breached his fiduciary duty of loyalty and good faith by secretly creating a competing organization to seize control of Noah House and exploiting the work already done by ABC Metro on developing the project. The second cause of action alleges that SHF and its Executive Director Lamberg, as consultants hired by ABC Metro, breached their duty of good faith in that, after being involved in negotiating for the purchase of the property from Great Wall, SHF and Lamberg attempted to take control of both the project and the property. The third cause of action asserts a breach of contract claim against SHF based on the same allegations. The fourth and fifth causes of action are asserted against Galloway and against SHF and Lamberg, respectively, for diversion of corporate opportunity.

An agent may not divert or exploit for his own benefit an opportunity that is an asset of his principal. * * * Nor may he make use of the principal's resources or proprietary information to organize a competing business. It would be a breach of fiduciary duty if an agent of a corporation secretly established a competing entity so as to divert opportunities away from his principal.

In support of dismissal, Galloway argues that he owed no fiduciary duty to ABC Metro because he was an employee of the Flemister entities, not of ABC Metro. To the contrary, the facts as alleged in the complaint indicate that he was acting as ABC Metro's agent with respect to Noah House, in addition to whatever services he performed for the Flemister entities. Moreover, he cannot have it both ways: to defeat the Flemister plaintiffs' standing, he asserts that they had no relation to his work on Noah House, but to defeat ABC Metro's claims, he asserts that he was the Flemisters' agent. At the very least, this inconsistency concerning the relationship between the parties must be resolved in further proceedings.

* * *

With respect to all causes of action asserted against them in their capacity as directors of CLC, Lambert and Harwood argue that they have immunity under Not-For-Profit Corporation Law § 720-a as uncompensated directors of a not-for-profit corporation. Yet, the statute contains an exception where the director's harmful conduct was grossly negligent or intentional. It would be premature to find that Lamberg and Harwood have immunity as a matter of law, since ABC Metro has alleged in detail that these defendants formed CLC so as to assist Galloway's deceptive scheme and appropriate the Great Wall property for themselves. This would come within the statutory exception for intentional misconduct.

Accordingly, the order of the Supreme Court, New York County (Ira Gammerman, J.), entered November 13, 1998, granting defendants' motion to dismiss the amended complaint, should be modified, on the law, to reinstate the first through ninth and the eleventh through sixteenth causes of action, only to the extent asserted by plaintiff American Baptist Churches of Metropolitan New York, and otherwise affirmed, without costs.

All concur.

D. ENFORCEMENT OF FIDUCIARY OBLIGATIONS

4. DONORS

Page 272:

At the end of the carryover paragraph, insert:

1A. Heirs of Donors' Rights. In Smithers v. St. Luke's-Roosevelt Hospital Center, 723 N.Y.S.2d 426 (Sup. Ct. App. Div. 2001), the widow of the donor of a charitable gift that established an alcoholism treatment center run by the defendant hospital was granted standing to sue to enforce the terms of the contribution. In 1971, R. Brinkley Smithers, a recovering alcoholic, pledged $10 million for the establishment of the Smithers Alcoholism Treatment Center. With the first $1 million, the hospital purchased a mansion in Manhattan to house the rehabilitation program. Smithers remained involved in the management and affairs of the program, and though the relationship was sometimes strained he completed his pledge. Smithers died in 1994, and one year later the hospital announced its plans to move the center into a hospital ward and sell the mansion. In 1995 Mrs. Smithers discovered the hospital had transferred funds from the Smithers Endowment to its general fund in violation of the gift. The widow, appointed special testatrix of the Smithers estate for the purpose of pursuing the claim, sought to enjoin the sale of the building and to obtain an accounting. Although two successive administrations of attorneys general entered certificate of discontinuances with the Hospital, the court held that though the attorney general represented ultimate charitable beneficiaries, it was not the exclusive representative of donors of charitable gifts. One judge dissented.

CHAPTER 4

REGULATION OF CHARITABLE SOLICITATION

B. CONSTITUTIONAL RESTRICTIONS ON REGULATION

Page 304:

After the third full paragraph, insert:

3A.   Professional Fundraisers' Bonding Requirements.   In an important decision interpreting a state's right to regulate professional fundraisers, the U.S. Court of Appeals for the Tenth Circuit struck down several provisions of Utah's Charitable Solicitations Act but upheld other sections including registration and annual fee requirements, and disclosure mandates. American Target Advertising v. Giani, 199 F.3d 1241 (10th Cir. 2000), cert. denied, 121 S.Ct.34 (2000). American Target offers fundraising services to nonprofit organizations. Controlled by Richard Viguerie, a former fundraiser for conservative political candidates, American Target had a contract with a nonprofit, Judicial Watch, to manage its national direct mail campaign. By virtue of this contract, American Target was classified as a professional fundraising consultant under the Utah Charitable Solicitations Act, which required all such consultants to register with the state, obtain a permit, pay an annual fee of $250 and post a bond or letter of credit in the amount of $25,000.

American Target challenged the Solicitations Act as an impermissible abridgement of protected speech and as an unconstitutional prior restraint. The Court found that the registration and disclosure provisions clearly targeted fraud and enabled Utah citizens to make informed decisions concerning their charitable donations. The bond requirement, however, was found to support a different state interest, providing a victim relief fund for those injured through violations of the Act which only peripherally supported the recognized interest in regulatory oversight. American Target maintained it did not have sufficient unpledged collateral on hand to secure the bond.   The Court held that this provision unnecessarily interfered with First Amendment freedoms and only peripherally supported the state interest in regulatory oversight. It also struck down as prior restraints the provisions which gave the Director of the Division of Consumer Protection the power to request "any additional information the division may require," the power to deny a permit if the applicant has failed reasonably to supervise its agents, or employees, solicitors, or fundraising counsel. The court found that the state official had impermissible uncontrolled discretion to deny, suspend or revoke an application, registration, permit or information card which created an unacceptable risk of the suppression of ideas.

PART THREE

TAXATION OF
NONPROFIT ORGANIZATIONS

CHAPTER 5

TAX EXEMPTION: PUBLIC BENEFIT
ORGANIZATIONS

C. BASIC REQUIREMENTS FOR CHARITABLE TAX EXEMPTION

3. THE PUBLIC POLICY LIMITATION

Page 382:

At the end of Note 10 (For Further Reading), add:

David A. Brennen, The Power of the Treasury: Racial Discrimination, Public Policy, and "Charity" in Contemporary Society, 33 U.C.Davis L. Rev. 389 (2000).

7. OTHER EXEMPT PURPOSES

Page 456:

At the end of the carryover paragraph, add:

For a recent case on amateur baseball as an exempt purpose, see Wayne Baseball, Inc. v. Commissioner, 78 T.C.M. 437 (1999), where the Tax Court found that more than an insubstantial part of an amateur baseball team's activities furthered the nonexempt social and recreational interests of its members. Unlike the Hutchinson Broncos, the team in *Wayne Baseball* did not promote amateur athletics by providing instruction or facilities to the community or engaging in other charitable activities.

D. COMMERCIAL ACTIVITIES AND JOINT VENTURES

2. JOINT VENTURES

Page 493:

After the first full paragraph, insert:

Those who were expecting meaningful appellate court guidance on joint ventures from the Ninth Circuit's widely anticipated opinion in *Redlands Surgical Services* were sorely disappointed. In a per curiam opinion issued a mere ten days after oral argument, the court affirmed the Tax Court's decision, noting briefly that it was specifically adopting the trial court holding that RSS had ceded effective control over the operations of the partnerships and the surgery center to private parties, conferring impermissible private benefit. Redlands Surgical Services v. Commissioner, 242 F.3d 904 (9th Cir. 2001). It is highly unlikely that the Supreme Court would grant certiorari in this case if it is requested by the taxpayer.

E. INUREMENT, PRIVATE BENEFIT AND INTERMEDIATE SANCTIONS

1. INUREMENT AND PRIVATE BENEFIT

Page 510:

After the fourth full paragraph, insert:

1A. *The Final Episode: United Cancer Council Settlement.* The Tax Court was deprived of the opportunity to reconsider the *United Cancer Council* case on remand when in February, 2000, the IRS and UCC settled their longstanding exemption dispute. UCC, which had filed for bankruptcy, conceded that it was not entitled to exemption under § 501(c)(3) for the years 1986-1989, and the IRS restored UCC's exemption from 1990 forward. As a condition to the settlement, UCC agreed to stop raising funds from the general public and to limit its activities to accepting charitable bequests and transmitting them to local cancer councils for direct care of patients.

Although no Tax Court guidance will be forthcoming on the private benefit issue in *UCC*, its precedential value would have been minimal in any event because the IRS's focus has shifted away from the inurement and private benefit doctrines with the enactment of the § 4958 intermediate sanctions regime. See Note 2, infra, at casebook p. 510. For a discussion of the UCC settlement, see Carolyn D. Wright, UCC, IRS Settle Decade-Long Exemption Dispute: 501(c)(3) Status

Revoked for Three Years, 28 Exempt Org. Tax Rev. 189 (2000). For the text of the settlement agreement, see 28 Exempt Org. Tax Rev. 250 (2000).

2. INTERMEDIATE SANCTIONS ON EXCESS BENEFIT TRANSACTIONS

Page 518:

Delete the first full paragraph, and insert:

Temporary Regulations. Instead of promulgating final intermediate sanctions regulations, as predicted in the text, the Service issued a lengthy set of temporary regulations on January 10, 2001.[1] The temporary regulations are similar in many respects to the earlier proposed regulations, but they also respond to numerous comments and criticisms from practitioners and exempt organizations. This Note is a selective survey of the major changes. Many small details and transitional rules have been omitted from this discussion. The full text of the temporary regulations has been reproduced in the Appendix, *infra* this Supplement, at pp. 78 et seq.

Applicable Tax-Exempt Organization. Section 4958 applies only to "applicable" § 501(c)(3) and § 501(c)(4) organizations, including organizations that were exempt under either of those sections at any time during a five-year lookback period ending on the date of any excess benefit transaction under scrutiny. Temp. Treas. Reg. § 53.4958-2T(a). In response to queries from commentators, the temporary regulations provide that governmental entities whose income tax exemption derives from § 115 -- e.g., state colleges or universities -- are not subject to the § 4958 regime even if they also voluntarily applied for (and received) an exemption under § 501(c)(3). Id.

Definition of Disqualified Person. The temporary regulations make it clear that the vast majority of employees and independent contractors who render services to § 501(c)(3) and § 501(c)(4) organizations are not disqualified persons (DQPs) and thus will not be subject to penalties under § 4958. In clarifying how to identify those persons who have the level of substantial influence to be DQPs, the temporary regulations offer the following additional guidance:

> (1) Those persons who are in a position to have substantial influence because of their status as officers, directors, trustees, and the like will

---

[1] T.D. 8920, REG-246256-96. Unlike proposed regulations, temporary regulations have the same legal force and effect as final regulations for up to three years. The Service may continue to solicit comments and suggestions until the final version is released.

be categorized as DQPs only by virtue of their actual powers and responsibilities, not merely by their title. Temp. Treas. Reg. § 53.4958-3T(c). Thus, individuals holding the title of "director" or even "president" would not be a DQP if in reality they had no powers or ultimate responsibility.

(2) Section 501(c)(3) organizations, including private foundations, will not be DQPs (with respect to other organizations, for example, with whom they might be affiliated), nor will § 501(c)(4) organizations with respect to transactions with other (c)(4)'s. Temp. Treas. Reg. § 53.4958-3T(d)(1) & (2). This leaves open the possibility that a "(c)(4)" may be a DQP with respect to transactions with a related "(c)(3)" organization.

(3) A person's status as a "substantial contributor" to an organization (borrowing the definition in § 507(a)(2)) may be a factor demonstrating substantial influence, but only contributions received by the organization during its current taxable year and the four preceding taxable years are taken into account for this purpose. Temp. Treas. Reg. § 53.4958-3T(e)(2)(ii).[2]

(4) With respect to factors tending to show that a person does or does not have substantial influence, independent contractor status (e.g., as an attorney, accountant and investment adviser whose sole relationship to the organization is rendering professional advice but who does not have decisionmaking authority with respect to transactions from which no personal economic benefit will be derived other than customary fees) is a factor tending to show no substantial influence. Temp. Treas. Reg. § 53.4958-3T(e)(3)(ii); see also Temp. Treas. Reg. § 53.4958-3T(g) Example 12.

(5) Two additional factors were added that "tend to show" the absence of substantial influence: (a) the individual's direct supervisor is not a DQP, and (b) the person does not participate in any management decisions affecting the organization as a whole or a discrete segment or activity of the organization that represents a substantial portion of its activities, assets, income or expenses. Temp. Treas. Reg. § 53.4958-3T(e)(3)(iii), (iv).

Initial Contract Exception. It had been unclear whether persons with no prior relationship to an organization could be a DQP with respect to their first

---

[2]Generally, a "substantial contributor" is a donor who has contributed or bequeathed more than $5,000 to an organization if that amount exceeds 2% of the total contributions and bequests received by the organization at any time through the close of the current taxable year.

contractual relationship, or whether first-timers should be protected from intermediate sanctions by a "one-free-bite" rule. The temporary regulations address this question with a significant new initial contract exception crafted in response to the decision in United Cancer Council v. Commissioner, *supra* casebook, p. 503, where the Seventh Circuit held that inurement of private gain cannot result from a contractual relationship entered into at arm's length between an exempt organization and a party having no prior relationship with the organization. Although *United Cancer Council* was not a § 4958 case and did not involve the technical definition of DQP, it influenced the Service to conclude that a one-free bite rule was appropriate in certain situations.

The temporary regulations generally provide that § 4958 does not apply to any fixed payment made to a person with respect to an initial contract, regardless of whether the payment would otherwise constitute an EBT. Temp. Treas. Reg. § 53.4958-4T(a)(3)(i). For this purpose, an "initial contract" is a binding written contract between an exempt organization and a person who was not a DQP immediately prior to entering into the contract. Temp. Treas. Reg. § 53.4958-4T(a)(3)(iii). A "fixed payment" is an amount of cash or other property specified in the contract or determined by a specified objective "fixed formula" (e.g., a nondiscretionary bonus based on future revenue generated by the organization's activities), which is to be paid or transferred in exchange for the provision of specified services or property. Temp. Treas. Reg. § 53.4958-4T(a)(3)(ii). If an initial contract provides for both fixed and non-fixed (e.g., discretionary) payments, the fixed payments will not be subject to § 4958 while the non-fixed payments may be scrutinized, taking into account the DQP's entire compensation package. Temp. Treas. Reg. § 53.4958-4T(a)(3)(vi).

The theory of the initial contract exception is that a person who negotiates in good faith before he is in a position to exercise substantial influence should not be subject to sanctions even if the consideration received turns out to be excessive. But immunity is not considered to be appropriate with respect to payments where future discretion must be exercised (and thus may be subject to the DQP's substantial influence) in calculating the amount or deciding whether to make a payment. For 11 examples illustrating the application of the initial contract rule, see Temp. Treas. Reg. § 53.4958-4T(a)(3)(vii).

Excess Benefit Transactions. The temporary regulations elaborate on the definition of an excess benefit transaction ("EBT") and delineate certain specific items that either are disregarded or must be taken into account in determining the value of a compensation package.

In response to requests from commentators, the temporary regulations clarify the definition of an indirect EBT. They provide, for example, that an exempt organization may provide an economic benefit to a DQP indirectly either through a controlled subsidiary or an intermediary, with "control" measured by a 50%

benchmark and "intermediary" being defined as any person (including entities) who "participate" in a transaction with one or more DQPs in an attempt to "launder" the benefit. Temp. Treas. Reg. § 53.4958-4T(a)(2)(i)-(iii). For four examples of indirect self-dealing, see Temp. Treas. Reg. § 53.4958-4T(a)(2)(iv).

Modifying some of the rules discussed in the text, the temporary regulations also clarify the economic benefits that for ease of administration are disregarded for § 4958 purposes. Significantly, with limited exceptions relating to payment of liability insurance premiums, all fringe benefits excluded from income under § 132 are disregarded. Temp. Treas. Reg. § 53.4958-4T(a)(4)(i). In another important clarification, the regulations make it clear that although an exempt organization's payment of premiums for liability insurance and indemnification of officers, directors or trustees against civil liability are considered as compensation in evaluating the overall reasonableness of a DQP's compensation for § 4958 purposes, such inclusion is not determinative of whether or not the benefit is included in the DQP's gross income for income tax purposes (and, in most cases, it is not included). Temp. Treas. Reg. § 53.4958-4T(b)(1)(ii)(C).

To monitor disguised compensation, § 4958(c)(1)(A) and the proposed regulations provided that an economic benefit would not be treated as consideration for services for § 4958 purposes unless the exempt organization clearly indicates its intent (through "clear and convincing evidence") to treat the benefits as compensation -- e.g., on an original or amended tax information return such as a W-2 or 1099. A clear indication of intent to treat an employee benefit as part of a reasonable compensation package is desirable because it will avoid any sanctionable excess benefit. The temporary regulations permit a DQP who discovers a failure to manifest the requisite intent to amend his or her federal income tax return to report a benefit as income at any time prior to when the Service commences an audit of the DQP or the exempt organization. Temp. Treas. Reg. § 53.4958-45(c)(3)(i)(B). The temporary regulations also drop any reference to "clear and convincing evidence" and provide instead that an organization must provide "written substantiation that is contemporaneous with the transfer of benefits at issue." Temp. Treas. Reg. § 53.4958-4T(c)(1). This rule is coupled with a safe harbor under which an applicable exempt organization is not required to substantiate its intent to provide an economic benefit as compensation if the benefit is excluded from the DQP's income for income tax purposes. Temp. Treas. Reg. § 53.4958-4T(c)(2). As a result, although qualified pension and other nontaxable benefits must be taken into account in determining if compensation is reasonable (unless specifically disregarded -- e.g., de minimis and certain other fringe benefits excluded under § 132), they are not subject to the contemporaneous written substantiation requirement. All of this is supposed to make it easier for exempt organizations, but the regulations are sufficiently detailed and technical that moderately sophisticated tax advice will be required to follow the regulatory roadmap.

Revenue-Sharing Transactions. The temporary regulations continue to punt on the special rules applicable to revenue-sharing transactions. Temp. Treas. Reg. § 53.4958-5T. The Treasury will continue to consider comments. In the meantime, revenue-sharing transactions will be evaluated under the general rules defining EBTs, leaving a fog of uncertainty.

Rebuttable Presumption of Reasonableness. The temporary regulations offer some new clarification regarding the three requirements for invoking the rebuttable presumption of reasonableness. The director of the IRS's Exempt Organizations Division has characterized this guidance as a "step-by-step, 'cookbook' procedure" -- a "recipe" requiring some time and effort to follow that in the end will be relatively easy in most cases and will give comfort to exempt organizations and their DQPs. Steven T. Miller, Easier Compliance is Goal of New Intermediate Sanctions Regulations, reprinted in 31 Exempt Org. Tax Rev. 342 (2001).

The temporary regulations retain the requirement that those individuals on the governing body (or committee) who approve the transaction must be entirely free of any conflict of interest with respect to the compensation arrangement or property transfer. Temp. Treas. Reg. § 53.4958-6T(a)(1). It is not sufficient for a board member merely to disclose his or her conflict and participate if nobody objects. The regulations also purport to offer flexibility on the type of comparability data on which the governing body may rely. One frequently expressed concern was that a customized (and expensive) independent compensation report was required in all cases not protected by the small organization safe harbor for small organizations. The regulations give far more leeway, requiring broadly that a governing body has appropriate comparability data if, given the knowledge and expertise of its members, it has information sufficient to determine whether the compensation arrangement is reasonable or a property transfer is at fair market value. Temp. Treas. Reg. § 53.4958-6T(c)(2)(i). This would permit the use of a less customized or internally developed data, such as an industry compensation survey or even documented phone calls, as long as the comparables were relevant to the position under scrutiny. See, e.g., Temp. Treas. Reg. § 53.4958-6T(c)(iv) Examples.

For organizations with average annual gross receipts of less than $1 million, the regulations provide additional relief by permitting these smaller nonprofits to rely on data obtained from three (down from five) comparable organizations. Temp. Treas. Reg. § 53.4958-6T(c)(2)(ii).

A stricter rule is provided in applying the rebuttable presumption to "non-fixed" payments, such as a discretionary bonus. In general, unless a fixed formula for calculating the payment is specified at the outset, no rebuttable presumption arises until the exact amount of the payment is determined, and the three requirements for the presumption must be satisfied at that time. Temp. Treas. Reg. § 53.4958-6T(d)(1). But if the governing body approves an employment contract with a DQP that includes a non-fixed payment with a specified cap on the amount, the rebuttable presumption may be established at the time the contract is entered into by assuming, in effect, that the maximum amount payable under the contract will be paid and by satisfying the requirements giving rise to the rebuttable presumption for that maximum amount. Temp. Treas. Reg. § 53.4958-6T(d)(2).

Correction. The temporary regulations provide clarification on the steps necessary to correct an EBT, covering such details as how to calculate the interest on the excess benefit amount, the appropriate forms of correction, and the special problems presented by deferred compensation plans or where the applicable tax-exempt organization no longer exists at the time correction is required. For the details on this and much more, see Temp. Treas. Reg. § 53.4958-7T.

Effect of Intermediate Sanctions on Exempt Status. The earlier proposed regulations did not include any discussion of the relationship of intermediate sanctions penalties on an exempt organization's exempt status. As noted in the main text, the preamble listed some factors to be considered in determining whether and when revocation was appropriate, but the Service's failure to address this issue more directly in the regulations was criticized by commentators.

The Service continues to hedge because of a legitimate concern that § 4958 was not intended to affect the substantive standards (e.g., inurement and private benefit) for tax exemption under § 501(c)(3) or § 501(c)(4). The temporary regulations state this explicitly, without much elaboration (Temp. Reg. § 53.4958-8T(a)), and the preamble simply states that the Service intends to continue exercising administrative discretion in enforcing this area of the law and will publish guidance concerning the factors that will influence its discretion as it gains more experience administering the § 4958 regime. In other words, stay tuned.

Page 519:

Delete Problem (d) and insert the following new problem:

(d) Private University ("University") hires Coach for an initial term as head coach of its highly successful men's collegiate basketball team. They agree to a three-year employment contract, with the following elements: $400,000 base salary paid by the University; an additional $100,000 paid by University's separately incorporated alumni association; a $50,000 bonus if the basketball team advances beyond the first round of the NCAA Tournament; and free use of a car, a country club membership, and a standard fringe benefit package (including medical and disability insurance and a qualified pension plan). University expects that Coach's presence will greatly increase fundraising and also agrees to pay him an amount equal to five percent of the gross amount

*need
mounts will
be more highly
scrutinyed*

raised for the basketball program. Finally, Coach receives an additional $500,000 pursuant to a contract with a for-profit company that provides shoes and other athletic apparel for use by student-athletes at University. What if the employment contract and other benefits were in connection with a five-year contract renewal? Would the analysis be any different if Coach was employed by a state university?

F. LIMITATIONS ON LOBBYING AND POLITICAL CAMPAIGN ACTIVITY

5. POLITICAL CAMPAIGN LIMITATIONS

Page 560:

Remove the district court opinion in *Branch Ministries v. Rossotti*, and replace it with:

BRANCH MINISTRIES v. ROSSOTTI

United States Court of Appeals, District of Columbia Circuit, 2000.
211 F.3d 137.

BUCKLEY, Senior Judge:

facts

Four days before the 1992 presidential election, Branch Ministries, a tax-exempt church, placed full-page advertisements in two newspapers in which it urged Christians not to vote for then-presidential candidate Bill Clinton because of his positions on certain moral issues. The Internal Revenue Service concluded that the placement of the advertisements violated the statutory restrictions on organizations exempt from taxation and, for the first time in its history, it revoked a bona fide church's tax-exempt status because of its involvement in politics. Branch Ministries and its pastor, Dan Little, challenge the revocation on the grounds that (1) the Service acted beyond its statutory authority, (2) the revocation violated its right to the free exercise of religion guaranteed by the First Amendment and the Religious Freedom Restoration Act, and (3) it was the victim of selective prosecution in violation of the Fifth Amendment. Because these objections are without merit, we affirm the district court's grant of summary judgment to the Service.

I. BACKGROUND

A. Taxation of Churches

The Internal Revenue Code ("Code") exempts certain organizations from taxation, including those organized and operated for religious purposes, provided that they do not engage in certain activities, including involvement in "any political campaign on behalf of (or in opposition to) any candidate for public office." 26 U.S.C. § 501(a), (c)(3) (1994). Contributions to such organizations are also deductible from the donating taxpayer's taxable income. Id. § 170(a). Although most organizations seeking tax-exempt status are required to apply to the Internal Revenue Service ("IRS" or "Service") for an advance determination that they meet the requirements of section 501(c)(3), id. § 508(a), a church may simply hold itself out as tax exempt and receive the benefits of that status without applying for advance recognition from the IRS. Id. § 508(c)(1)(A).

The IRS maintains a periodically updated "Publication No. 78," in which it lists all organizations that have received a ruling or determination letter confirming the deductibility of contributions made to them. See Rev. Proc. 82-39, 1982-1 C.B. 759, §§ 2.01, 2.03. Thus, a listing in that publication will provide donors with advance assurance that their contributions will be deductible under section 170(a). If a listed organization has subsequently had its tax-exempt status revoked, contributions that are made to it by a donor who is unaware of the change in status will generally be treated as deductible if made on or before the date that the revocation is publicly announced. Id. § 3.01. Donors to a church that has not received an advance determination of its tax-exempt status may also deduct their contributions; but in the event of an audit, the taxpayer will bear the burden of establishing that the church meets the requirements of section 501(c)(3). See generally id. § 3.04; Rev. Proc. 80-24, 1980-1 C.B. 658, § 6 (discussing taxpayers' obligations in seeking a ruling or determination letter).

The unique treatment churches receive in the Internal Revenue Code is further reflected in special restrictions on the IRS's ability to investigate the tax status of a church. The Church Audit Procedures Act ("CAPA") sets out the circumstances under which the IRS may initiate an investigation of a church and the procedures it is required to follow in such an investigation. 26 U.S.C. § 7611. Upon a "reasonable belief" by a high-level Treasury official that a church may not be exempt from taxation under section 501, the IRS may begin a "church tax inquiry." Id. § 7611(a). A church tax inquiry is defined, rather circularly, as any inquiry to a church (other than an examination) to serve as a basis for determining whether a church- (A) is exempt from tax under section 501(a) by reason of its status as a church, or (B) is ... engaged in activities which may be subject to taxation.... Id. § 7611(h)(2). If the IRS is not able to resolve its concerns through a church tax inquiry, it may proceed to the second level of investigation: a "church tax examination." In such an examination, the IRS may obtain and review the church's records or examine its activities "to determine whether [the] organization claiming to be a church is a church for any period." Id. § 7611(b)(1)(A), (B).

B. Factual and Procedural History

Branch Ministries, Inc. operates the Church at Pierce Creek ("Church"), a Christian church located in Binghamton, New York. In 1983, the Church requested and received a letter from the IRS recognizing its tax-exempt status. On October 30, 1992, four days before the presidential election, the Church placed full-page advertisements in USA Today and the Washington Times. Each bore the headline "Christians Beware" and asserted that then-Governor Clinton's positions concerning abortion, homosexuality, and the distribution of condoms to teenagers in schools violated Biblical precepts. The following appeared at the bottom of each advertisement: This advertisement was co-sponsored by the Church at Pierce Creek, Daniel J. Little, Senior Pastor, and by churches and concerned Christians nationwide. Tax deductible donations for this advertisement gladly accepted. Make donations to: The Church at Pierce Creek. [mailing address]. * * *

The advertisements did not go unnoticed. They produced hundreds of contributions to the Church from across the country and were mentioned in a New York Times article and an Anthony Lewis column which stated that the sponsors of the advertisement had almost certainly violated the Internal Revenue Code. Peter Applebome, Religious Right Intensifies Campaign for Bush, N.Y. Times, Oct. 31, 1992, at A1; Anthony Lewis, Tax Exempt Politics?, N.Y. Times, Dec. 1, 1992, at A15.

The advertisements also came to the attention of the Regional Commissioner of the IRS, who notified the Church on November 20, 1992 that he had authorized a church tax inquiry based on "a reasonable belief ... that you may not be tax-exempt or that you may be liable for tax" due to political activities and expenditures. Letter from Cornelius J. Coleman, IRS Regional Commissioner, to The Church at Pierce Creek (Nov. 20, 1992), reprinted in App. at Tab 5, Ex. F. The Church denied that it had engaged in any prohibited political activity and declined to provide the IRS with certain information the Service had requested. On February 11, 1993, the IRS informed the Church that it was beginning a church tax examination. Following two unproductive meetings between the parties, the IRS revoked the Church's section 501(c)(3) tax-exempt status on January 19, 1995, citing the newspaper advertisements as prohibited intervention in a political campaign.

The Church and Pastor Little (collectively, "Church") commenced this lawsuit soon thereafter. This had the effect of suspending the revocation of the Church's tax exemption until the district court entered its judgment in this case. See 26 U.S.C. § 7428(c). The Church challenged the revocation of its tax-exempt status, alleging that the IRS had no authority to revoke its tax exemption, that the revocation violated its right to free speech and to freely exercise its religion under the First Amendment and the Religious Freedom Restoration Act of 1993, 42 U.S.C. § 2000bb (1994) ("RFRA"), and that the IRS engaged in selective prosecution in violation of the Equal Protection Clause of the Fifth Amendment. After allowing discovery on the Church's selective prosecution claim, Branch

Ministries, Inc. v. Richardson, 970 F.Supp. 11 (D.D.C.1997), the district court granted summary judgment in favor of the IRS. Branch Ministries, Inc. v. Rossotti, 40 F.Supp.2d 15 (D.D.C.1999).

The Church filed a timely appeal, and we have jurisdiction pursuant to 28 U.S.C. § 1291. We review summary judgment decisions de novo, see Everett v. United States, 158 F.3d 1364, 1367 (D.C.Cir.1998), cert. denied, 526 U.S. 1132, 119 S.Ct. 1807, 143 L.Ed.2d 1010 (1999), and will affirm only if there is no genuine issue as to any material fact and the moving party is entitled to judgment as a matter of law. Fed.R.Civ.P. 56(c).

II. ANALYSIS

The Church advances a number of arguments in support of its challenges to the revocation. We examine only those that warrant analysis.

A. The Statutory Authority of the IRS

The Church argues that, under the Internal Revenue Code, the IRS does not have the statutory authority to revoke the tax-exempt status of a bona fide church. It reasons as follows: section 501(c)(3) refers to tax-exempt status for religious organizations, not churches; section 508, on the other hand, specifically exempts "churches" from the requirement of applying for advance recognition of tax-exempt status, id. § 508(c)(1)(A); therefore, according to the Church, its tax-exempt status is derived not from section 501(c)(3), but from the lack of any provision in the Code for the taxation of churches. The Church concludes from this that it is not subject to taxation and that the IRS is therefore powerless to place conditions upon or to remove its tax-exempt status as a church.

We find this argument more creative than persuasive. The simple answer, of course, is that whereas not every religious organization is a church, every church is a religious organization. More to the point, irrespective of whether it was required to do so, the Church applied to the IRS for an advance determination of its tax-exempt status. The IRS granted that recognition and now seeks to withdraw it. CAPA gives the IRS this power.

That statute, which pertains exclusively to churches, provides authority for revocation of the tax-exempt status of a church through its references to other sections of the Internal Revenue Code. The section of CAPA entitled "Limitations on revocation of tax-exempt status, etc." provides that the Secretary [of the Treasury] may "determine that an organization is not a church which [ ] (i) is exempt from taxation by reason of section 501(a), or (ii) is described in section 170(c)." 26 U.S.C. § 7611(d)(1)(A)(i), (ii). Both of these sections condition tax-exempt status on non-intervention in political campaigns. Section 501(a) states that "[a]n organization described in subsection (c) ... shall be exempt from taxation...." Id. § 501(a). Those described in subsection (c) include corporations ... organized and operated exclusively for religious ... purposes ... which do[ ] not participate in, or intervene in (including the publishing or distributing of statements), any political campaign on behalf of (or in opposition to) any candidate for public office. Id. § 501(c)(3). Similarly, section 170(c) allows taxpayers to deduct from their taxable income donations made to a corporation organized and operated exclusively for religious ... purposes ... which is not disqualified for tax exemption under section 501(c)(3) by reason of attempting to ... intervene in (including the publishing or distributing of statements), any political campaign on behalf of (or in opposition to) any candidate for public office. Id. § 170(c)(2)(B), (D).

The Code, in short, specifically states that organizations that fail to comply with the restrictions set forth in section 501(c) are not qualified to receive the tax exemption that it provides. Having satisfied ourselves that the IRS had the statutory authority to revoke the Church's tax-exempt status, we now turn to the free exercise challenges.

B. First Amendment Claims and the RFRA

The Church claims that the revocation of its exemption violated its right to freely exercise its religion under both the First Amendment and the RFRA. To sustain its claim under either the Constitution or the statute, the Church must first establish that its free exercise right has been substantially burdened. See Jimmy Swaggart Ministries v. Board of Equalization, 493 U.S. 378, 384-85, 110 S.Ct. 688, 107 L.Ed.2d 796 (1990) ("Our cases have established that the free exercise inquiry asks whether government has placed a substantial burden on the observation of a central religious belief or practice and, if so, whether a compelling governmental interest justifies the burden.") (internal quotation marks and brackets omitted); 42 U.S.C. § 2000bb-1(a), (b) ("Government shall not substantially burden a person's exercise of religion" in the absence of a compelling government interest that is furthered by the least restrictive means.). We conclude that the Church has failed to meet this test.

The Church asserts, first, that a revocation would threaten its existence. See Affidavit of Dan Little dated July 31, 1995 at P 22, reprinted in App. at Tab 8 ("The Church at Pierce Creek will have to close due to the revocation of its tax exempt status, and the inability of congregants to deduct their contributions from their taxes."). The Church maintains that a loss of its tax-exempt status will not only make its members reluctant to contribute the funds essential to its survival, but may obligate the Church itself to pay taxes.

The Church appears to assume that the withdrawal of a conditional privilege for failure to meet the condition is in itself an unconstitutional burden on its free exercise right. This is true, however, only if the receipt of the privilege (in this case the tax exemption) is conditioned upon conduct proscribed by a religious faith, or ... denie[d] ... because of conduct mandated by religious belief, thereby putting substantial pressure on an adherent to modify his behavior and to violate his beliefs. Jimmy Swaggart Ministries, 493 U.S. at 391-92 (internal quotation marks and citation omitted). Although its advertisements reflected its religious convictions on certain questions of morality, the Church does not maintain that a withdrawal from electoral politics would violate its beliefs. The sole effect of the loss of the tax exemption will be to decrease the amount of money available to the Church for its religious practices. The Supreme Court has declared, however, that such a burden "is not constitutionally significant." Id. at 391; see also Hernandez v. Commissioner, 490 U.S. 680, 700, 109 S.Ct. 2136, 104 L.Ed.2d 766 (1989) (the "contention that an incrementally larger tax burden interferes with [ ] religious activities ... knows no limitation").

In actual fact, even this burden is overstated. Because of the unique treatment churches receive under the Internal Revenue Code, the impact of the revocation is likely to be more symbolic than substantial. As the IRS confirmed at oral argument, if the Church does not intervene in future political campaigns, it may hold itself out as a 501(c)(3) organization and receive all the benefits of that status. All that will have been lost, in that event, is the advance assurance of deductibility in the event a donor should be audited. See 26 U.S.C. § 508(c)(1)(A); Rev. Proc. 82-39 § 2.03. Contributions will remain tax deductible as long as donors are able to establish that the Church meets the requirements of section 501(c)(3).

Nor does the revocation necessarily make the Church liable for the payment of taxes. As the IRS explicitly represented in its brief and reiterated at oral argument, the revocation of the exemption does not convert bona fide donations into income taxable to the Church. See 26 U.S.C. § 102 ("Gross income does not include the value of property acquired by gift...."). Furthermore, we know of no authority, and counsel provided none, to prevent the Church from reapplying for a prospective determination of its tax-exempt status and regaining the advance assurance of deductibility—provided, of course, that it renounces future involvement in political campaigns.

We also reject the Church's argument that it is substantially burdened because it has no alternate means by which to communicate its sentiments about candidates for public office. In Regan v. Taxation With Representation, 461 U.S. 540, 552-53, 103 S.Ct. 1997, 76 L.Ed.2d 129 (1983) (Blackmun, J., concurring), three members of the Supreme Court stated that the availability of such an alternate means of communication is essential to the constitutionality of section 501(c)(3)'s restrictions on lobbying. The Court subsequently confirmed that this was an accurate description of its holding. See FCC v. League of Women Voters, 468 U.S. 364, 400, 104 S.Ct. 3106, 82 L.Ed.2d 278 (1984). In Regan, the concurring justices noted that "TWR may use its present § 501(c)(3) organization for its nonlobbying activities and may create a § 501(c)(4) affiliate to pursue its charitable goals through lobbying." 461 U.S. at 552.

The Church has such an avenue available to it. As was the case with TWR, the Church may form a related organization under section 501(c)(4) of the Code. See 26 U.S.C. § 501(c)(4) (tax exemption for "[c]ivic leagues or organizations not organized for profit but operated exclusively for the promotion of social welfare"). Such organizations are exempt from taxation; but unlike their section 501(c)(3) counterparts, contributions to them are not deductible. See 26 U.S.C. § 170(c); see also Regan, 461 U.S. at 543, 552-53. Although a section 501(c)(4) organization is also subject to the ban on intervening in political campaigns, see 26 C.F.R. § 1.501(c)(4)-1(a)(2)(ii) (1999), it may form a political action committee ("PAC") that would be free to participate in political campaigns. Id. § 1.527-6(f), (g) ("[A]n organization described in section 501(c) that is exempt from taxation under section 501(a) may, [if it is not a section 501(c)(3) organization], establish and maintain such a separate segregated fund to receive contributions and make expenditures in a political campaign.").

At oral argument, counsel for the Church doggedly maintained that there can be no "Church at Pierce Creek PAC." True, it may not itself create a PAC; but as we have pointed out, the Church can initiate a series of steps that will provide an alternate means of political communication that will satisfy the standards set by the concurring justices in Regan. Should the Church proceed to do so, however, it must understand that the related 501(c)(4) organization must be separately incorporated; and it must maintain records that will demonstrate that tax-deductible contributions to the Church have not been used to support the political activities conducted by the 501(c)(4) organization's political action arm. See 26 U.S.C. § 527(f)(3); 26 C.F.R. § 1.527-6(e), (f).

That the Church cannot use its tax-free dollars to fund such a PAC unquestionably passes constitutional muster. The Supreme Court has consistently held that, absent invidious discrimination, "Congress has not violated [an organization's] First Amendment rights by declining to subsidize its First Amendment activities." Regan, 461 U.S. at 548; see also Cammarano v. United States, 358 U.S. 498, 513, 79 S.Ct. 524, 3 L.Ed.2d 462 (1959) ("Petitioners are not being denied a tax deduction because they engage in constitutionally protected activities, but are simply being required to pay for those activities entirely out of their own pockets, as everyone else engaging in similar activities is required to do under the provisions of the Internal Revenue Code.").

Because the Church has failed to demonstrate that its free exercise rights have been substantially burdened, we do not reach its arguments that section 501(c)(3) does not serve a compelling government interest or, if it is indeed compelling, that revocation of its tax exemption was not the least restrictive means of furthering that interest.

Nor does the Church succeed in its claim that the IRS has violated its First Amendment free speech rights by engaging in viewpoint discrimination. The restrictions imposed by section 501(c)(3) are viewpoint neutral; they prohibit intervention in favor of all candidates for public office by all tax-exempt organizations, regardless of candidate, party, or viewpoint. Cf. Regan, 461 U.S. at 550-51 (upholding denial of tax deduction for lobbying activities, in spite of allowance of such deduction for veteran's groups).

C. Selective Prosecution (Fifth Amendment)

The Church alleges that the IRS violated the Equal Protection Clause of the Fifth Amendment by engaging in selective prosecution. In support of its claim, the Church has submitted several hundred pages of newspaper excerpts reporting political campaign activities in, or by the pastors of, other churches that have retained their tax-exempt status. These include reports of explicit endorsements of Democratic candidates by clergymen as well as many instances in which favored candidates have been invited to address congregations from the pulpit. The Church complains that despite this widespread and widely reported involvement by other churches in political campaigns, it is the only one to have ever had its tax-exempt status revoked for engaging in political activity. It attributes this alleged discrimination to the Service's political bias.

To establish selective prosecution, the Church must "prove that (1) [it] was singled out for prosecution from among others similarly situated and (2) that [the] prosecution was improperly motivated, i.e., based on race, religion or another arbitrary classification." United States v. Washington, 705 F.2d 489, 494 (D.C.Cir.1983). This burden is a demanding one because "in the absence of clear evidence to the contrary, courts presume that [government prosecutors] have properly discharged their official duties." United States v. Armstrong, 517 U.S. 456, 464, 116 S.Ct. 1480, 134 L.Ed.2d 687 (1996) (internal quotation marks and citation omitted).

At oral argument, counsel for the IRS conceded that if some of the church-sponsored political activities cited by the Church were accurately reported, they were in violation of section 501(c)(3) and could have resulted in the revocation of those churches' tax-exempt status. But even if the Service could have revoked their tax exemptions, the Church has failed to establish selective prosecution because it has failed to demonstrate that it was similarly situated to any of those other churches. None of the reported activities involved the placement of advertisements in newspapers with nationwide circulations opposing a candidate and soliciting tax deductible contributions to defray their cost. As we have stated, [i]f ... there was no one to whom defendant could be compared in order to resolve the question of [prosecutorial] selection, then it follows that defendant has failed to make out one of the elements of its case. Discrimination cannot exist in a vacuum; it can be found only in the unequal treatment of people in similar circumstances. Attorney Gen. v. Irish People, Inc., 684 F.2d 928, 946 (D.C.Cir.1982); see also United States v. Hastings, 126 F.3d 310, 315 (4th Cir.1997) ("[D]efendants are similarly situated when their circumstances present no distinguishable legitimate prosecutorial factors that might justify making different prosecutorial decisions with respect to them.") (internal quotation marks and citation omitted).

Because the Church has failed to establish that it was singled out for prosecution from among others who were similarly situated, we need not examine whether the IRS was improperly motivated in undertaking this prosecution.

III. CONCLUSION

For the foregoing reasons, we find that the revocation of the Church's tax-exempt status neither violated the Constitution nor exceeded the IRS's statutory authority. The judgment of the district court is therefore

Affirmed.

Page 571:

At the bottom of the page, insert:

6A. USE OF THE INTERNET FOR LOBBYING AND OTHER POLITICAL ACTIVITIES

In Announcement 2000-84, 2000-42 I.R.B. 385, the Service requested comments on areas for which guidance was necessary to clarify the application of federal tax law to use of the Internet by exempt organizations. With the explosive growth of the Internet as a communications medium, the scope of this request was wide ranging. Three areas where the need for guidance is particularly compelling are: (1) lobbying and political activities; (2) the unrelated business income tax (see infra this Supplement p.38); and (3) charitable contributions (see infra this Supplement pp. 39-40). This Note, which assumes familiarity with Internet basics, highlights some of the major issues relating to lobbying and political activity.

Because it is a convenient and relatively inexpensive communications medium, the Internet has proven to be an effective vehicle for exempt organizations to lobby and otherwise attempt to influence the political process. The following examples, posed as hypothetical questions, illustrate the range of issues:

(1) A § 501(c)(3) educational organization with an advocacy mission that has not made the § 501(h) election devotes over half of its web site but a relatively insignificant portion of its budget to grassroots lobbying. How is this lobbying activity evaluated in applying the "no substantial part"

test? Is the location of the lobbying communication (e.g., home page or several clicks away) or number of hits relevant in making the "substantial part" determination?

(2)   A § 501(c)(3) charity that has made the § 501(h) lobbying election maintains an extensive (but inexpensive) web site that includes (in a prominent place) all the elements of grassroots lobbying communications on a wide range of issues. Alternatively, the various elements are spread around separate locations on the web site, but navigation is easy (or not) for those with an interest in the issue. The site also contains links to the web sites of other non-§ 501(c)(3) exempt organizations, and those sites include calls to action that meet all the elements of grassroots lobbying. Variations abound, as do issues which include: (a) how to apply the definitions of lobbying to web site communications; (b) when do statements on a web site constitute a "call to action" or a mass media communication for purposes of the mass media rule in Treas. Reg. § 56.4911-2(b)(5)(ii); (c) under what circumstances should information transmitted on or from the Internet be treated as a favored member communication for purposes of the § 501(h) election regime; (d) when should statements on a linked web site be attributed back to the originating exempt organization; and (e) how should expenses of the web site be allocated to lobbying communications.

(3)   A § 501(c)(3) charity's web site includes, as part of the organization's educational mission, links to an affiliated § 501(c)(4) advocacy organization or, alternatively, to a § 527 political action committee for a candidate for public office. The web site contains no overt statements supporting or opposing candidates, but many of the links (reached with just one click) include statements (or voter guides, etc.) whose content clearly violates the political campaign limitations in § 501(c)(3). Can these links be treated as nonpartisan voter education? What is required to make them nonpartisan? What if a § 501(c)(3) educational organization and its § 501(c)(4) lobbying affiliate share a web site that includes, in the (c)(4)'s cyberspace, statements that are proper for the (c)(4) but would warrant revocation of the (c)(3)'s exemption?

Any guidance that is forthcoming from the Service should be grounded in the developed law, such as it is, regulating lobbying and political activities by § 501(c)(3) organizations. Thus, a voter's guide that passes muster under the Service's ruling policy should be similarly evaluated if it is communicated through a web site. Similarly, a well advised § 501(c)(3) organization should avoid including overt statements on its web site that support or oppose candidates for public office, but its exemption should not be threatened if the links to candidate sites are incident to a nonpartisan educational mission. Beyond these obvious principles, however, the trouble spots (e.g., impact of hyperlinks, allocation of expenses) raise challenging questions that in the end will best be resolved by regulations or published rulings containing bright line safe harbors with a facts and circumstances fallback focusing on the organization's objective intent.

7. NONTAX REGULATION OF POLITICAL ACTIVITIES

Page 577:

After the third full paragraph, insert:

NOTE: § 527 POLITICAL ORGANIZATIONS—
REPORTING AND DISCLOSURE REQUIREMENTS

As discussed briefly in the casebook (see p. 571), § 527 provides a form of limited tax-exempt status for "political organizations," a broad category embracing political parties, political action committees, and funds created to support candidates and causes at the federal, state and local levels. Section 527 organizations are exempt from federal income tax on contributions they receive, and donors are exempt from federal gift tax on their contributions. Net investment income of political organizations is taxable at the highest corporate income tax rate (currently 35 percent).

Unlike § 501(c) tax-exempt organizations, § 527 organizations have not been required to apply for their special exempt status or file annual Form 990 information returns. Section 527 organizations with taxable investment income must file an annual return (Form 1120-POL), which reports taxable income and deductible expenses but does not include information on the specific activities of the organization or the sources of its revenue. Tax returns filed by political organizations have not been subject to the public disclosure and inspection requirements applicable to § 501(c) organizations, and § 527 organizations that seek to influence federal campaigns by engaging in "express advocacy" must disclose their activities and contributors to the Federal Election Commission. As discussed in the casebook (see p. 573), however, "express advocacy" generally is limited to advocating the election or defeat of specific candidates for federal elective office by using the magic words "vote for" and "vote against," and thus many § 527 groups need not file reports with the FEC.

Beginning in the mid-1990's, political activists, exploiting inconsistencies in the tax and election laws, began to form § 527 organizations to funnel vast sums of unregulated "soft money" to benefit political causes and candidates through activities such as voter education and issue advocacy. The principal goals of these new stealth vehicles were to: (1) avoid public disclosure of their activities and sources of income under both tax and election laws, (2) avoid federal election law limits on contributions, and (3) allow donors to contribute unlimited amounts without the gift tax exposure that they would face if the contributions were made to a §501(c)(4) advocacy organization.

The emergence of § 527 organizations was the subject of some scholarly discourse during the 1998 election campaign. See, e.g., Frances R. Hill, Probing the Limits of Section 527 to Design a New Campaign Finance Vehicle, 22 Exempt Org. Tax Rev. 205 (1998). But it was not until the 2000 primary season that campaign finance reformers and the media began to expose these secretive groups as the loophole of choice for raising and spending unlimited amounts on political activity without any tax liability or disclosure obligation. See John M. Broder & Raymond Bonner, A Political Voice, Without Strings, N.Y. Times, March 29, 2000, at A1. Among the specific groups exposed by journalists and reform advocates were Republicans for Clean Air, which broadcast advertisements critical of Senator John McCain before the March 2000 Super Tuesday primaries and reportedly was financed by a major supporter of George W. Bush; Citizens for a Republican Congress, which was said to raise and spend $35 million on ads in competitive Congressional races; Business Leaders for Sensible Priorities, created by the founders of Ben and Jerry's ice cream to argue for less spending on weapons and more on education; and Peace Action, an antiwar group which raised $250,000 in seed money from a few anonymous donors to influence the policy debate in a handful of contested Congressional races. Id.; see also Common Cause, Under the Radar: The Attack of the "Stealth PACs" on Our Nation's Elections, available at < www.commoncause.org/publications/utr/ > .

In June, 2000, Congress responded by passing narrowly tailored legislation (H.R. 4762, 106th Cong., 2d Sess.) to require § 527 organizations to disclose their activities and donors. President Clinton signed the bill as this 2000 Supplement went to press, stating that "[t]oday's actions will stop special interests from using 527 status to hide their political spending behind a tax-exempt front group." Among other things, the legislation requires § 527 groups to: (1) notify the IRS within 24 hours of their creation; (2) file periodic reports (more frequently in election years) of their activities and expenses; and (3) disclose their contributors unless they are already required to do so with the Federal Election Commission. Sanctions, including monetary penalties and possible loss of exempt status, will be imposed for noncompliance. Expanded disclosure rules require the IRS to make all this information available to the public on the Internet.

Although this legislation will bring the most secretive § 527 groups into the sunshine, it does not extend to other tax-exempt organizations often used for political advocacy, such as § 501(c)(4) social welfare organizations, § 501(c)(5) labor unions, and § 501(c)(6) trade associations. Conservative opponents of campaign finance reform failed in their attempt to extend the expanded disclosure requirements (e.g., publicly identifying donors) to § 501(c) organizations. They were targeting liberal advocacy groups and labor unions that also receive soft money for political purposes but, unlike § 527 groups, may not exist solely to engage in political campaign activities. With the passage of legislation limited to § 527 groups, secret soft money likely will migrate back to § 501(c)(4) organizations and, possibly, even to § 501(c)(3) charities (under the guise of "education") and for-profit entities. Opponents of campaign finance reform also are threatening a constitutional challenge to the new disclosure rules in the courts.

For Further Reading. Frances R. Hill, Softer Money: Exempt Organizations and Campaign Finance, 32 Exempt Org. Tax Rev. 27 (2001); Martin A. Sullivan, More Disclosure From 501(c)'s: Poison Pill or Good Policy, 29 Exempt Org. Tax Rev. 10 (2000).

H. PROCEDURAL ISSUES

2. INFORMATION RETURN AND DISCLOSURE REQUIREMENTS

Page 585:

After the third full paragraph, insert:

Joint Committee on Taxation Disclosure Study. Despite recent reforms, calls for still greater public disclosure by exempt organizations continue to reverberate from Washington. A study published in January, 2000, by the Joint Committee on Taxation staff proposes that nearly every piece of paper exchanged between tax-exempt organizations and the IRS be made public with very few redactions. See Joint Committee on Taxation, Study of Present-Law Taxpayer Confidentiality and Disclosure Provisions as Required by Section 3802 of the Internal Revenue Service Restructuring and Reform Act of 1998, Volume II: Study of Disclosure Provisions Relating to Tax-Exempt Organizations (JCS-1-00), Jan. 28, 2000, reprinted in 27 Exempt Org. Tax Rev. 567 (2000).

The JCT proposals are based on the premise that the public interest is best served by greater disclosure of information relating to tax-exempt organizations. Full disclosure, in the JCT's view, generally outweighs privacy concerns by enabling the general public to provide greater oversight of exempt organization activities, and it assists donors in determining whether organizations should be supported and whether changes in the law are needed.

Among the more significant recommendations in the JCT study are:

- Form 990 should be revised to provide more information and should be designed to be more understandable by the public.

- All written determinations and background file documents involving tax-exempt organizations should be disclosed without redaction.

- The results of IRS audits and all settlement agreements with tax-exempt organizations should be disclosed.

- Applications for exempt status and supporting documents should be disclosed when the application is submitted.

- Exempt organizations should be required to disclose not just their basic Form 990 information return but also any Form 990-T reporting unrelated business taxable income, and any UBIT returns filed by affiliates.

- Whether or not they make the § 501(h) election, all public charities should be required to provide a general description of their lobbying activities, expenses for self-defense lobbying and expenses for nonpartisan study, analysis or research if a "call to action" is included.

- The IRS should have more authority to share audit information with nontax state officials and agencies that have jurisdiction over exempt organizations.

Although the Joint Committee's proposals have received scattered applause from a handful of long-time disclosure proponents, they have been met with an icy reception from the mainstream nonprofit sector. Among the concerns expressed are that the mandatory disclosure of audit files and closing agreements would have a chilling effect on the settlement process; releasing unredacted private rulings and background documents would invade the privacy of exempt organizations, curtail the letter ruling process, and contribute to the dissemination of misleading and inaccurate information by the press; and the disclosure of UBIT returns will give an unfair advantage to an exempt organization's privately owned for-profit competitors. Critics also have questioned whether it is good policy to enlist the general public as vigilantes, as opposed to the IRS and other governmental agencies, to oversee the activities of the nonprofit sector. For a thoughtful critique of the JCT study, see Peter L. Faber, The Joint Committee Staff Disclosure Recommendations: What They Mean for Exempt Organizations, 28 Exempt Org. Tax Rev. 31 (2000).

CHAPTER 6

PRIVATE FOUNDATIONS

A. THE UNIVERSE OF PRIVATE FOUNDATIONS

2. THE DISTINCTION BETWEEN PRIVATE FOUNDATIONS AND PUBLIC CHARITIES: HISTORICAL ORIGINS

Page 620:

At the end of Note 2 (For Further Reading), add:

Thomas A. Troyer, The 1969 Private Foundation Law: Historical Perspectives on Its Origins and Underpinnings, 27 Exempt Org. Tax Rev. 52 (2000).

5. PRIVATE FOUNDATION ALTERNATIVES

Page 637:

At the end of the first full paragraph, insert:

Page 637:

At the end of the second full paragraph (For Further Reading), add:

Victoria B. Bjorklund, Charitable Giving to a Private Foundation: The Alternatives, The Supporting Organization, and the Donor-Advised Fund, 27 Exempt Org. Tax Rev. 107 (2000).

B. AVOIDING PRIVATE FOUNDATION STATUS

6. PROCEDURAL ASPECTS

b. INFORMATION REPORTING AND DISCLOSURE REQUIREMENTS

Page 670:

At the end of the third full paragraph, insert:

In January, 2000, the Service issued final regulations governing the public disclosure of private foundation annual information returns and exemption applications. T.D. 8861, 65 Fed. Reg. 2030 (Jan. 12, 2000). These regulations, which took effect on March 13, 2000, are very similar to the generally applicable disclosure rules governing other exempt organizations required to file Form 990 with the exception that private foundations, unlike public charities, must disclose the names and addresses of their contributors. Under the final regulations, a private foundation must provide copies of its three most recent annual information returns and its exemption application in response to an in-person request or within 30 days of receipt of a written request. For returns filed after March 13, 2000, private foundations no longer are required to publish a notice in a local newspaper announcing that their information return is available for inspection.

A more significant development on the disclosure front has been the posting on the Internet of the latest tax information returns for virtually every U.S. private foundation. The full collection of over 61,000 Form 990-PFs is available to scholars, grantseekers, journalists and voyeurs thanks to a joint project of Philanthropic Research, Inc. and the Urban Institute's National Center for Charitable Statistics. Their respective web sites are: <www.guidestar.org> and <www.nccs.urban.org>. The Form 990's of many public charities are also being posted on these two sites. Form 990's and other financial information for California charities are available on the California Attorney General's web site: <caag.state.ca.us/charities/>.

CHAPTER 7

TAX EXEMPTION: MUTUAL BENEFIT ORGANIZATIONS

C. TRADE ASSOCIATIONS AND OTHER BUSINESS LEAGUES

3. LOBBYING AND OTHER POLITICAL ACTIVITIES

Page 728:

At the end of the last paragraph, insert:

The constitutional challenge to §§ 162(e) and 6033(e) also was rejected by the D.C. Circuit, which affirmed the district court's decision. American Society of Association Executives v. United States, 195 F.3d 47 (D.C. Cir. 1999). Applying "rational basis" scrutiny, the court held that the challenged provisions did not violate First Amendment free speech rights or discriminate against organizations that lobby because the statutory scheme bore a rational relationship to the legislative goal of eliminating any tax subsidy for lobbying and preventing taxpayers from circumventing that goal. In finding no free speech burden, the court emphasized that a § 501(c)(6) organization could avoid any obligation to allocate dues or pay a proxy tax by dividing itself into two separate tax-exempt entities, one of which engages exclusively in lobbying and one that completely refrains from lobbying.

CHAPTER 8

THE UNRELATED BUSINESS INCOME TAX

B. NATURE OF AN UNRELATED TRADE OR BUSINESS

2. TAXABLE AND EXCEPTED ACTIVITIES

Page 797:

After the second full paragraph, insert:

In February, 2000, the IRS released proposed regulations on corporate sponsorship payments received by exempt organizations. These regulations replace the earlier 1993 version discussed in the text and generally are faithful to the language and legislative history of § 513(i). The full text of the proposed regulations had been reproduced in the Appendix, infra this Supplement at pp. 58-65.

The proposed regulations provide useful new guidance in several areas, including:

(1) Activities covered by the qualified sponsorship payment ("QSP") exclusion may include a single event (such as a bowl game, walkathon or television program); a series of related events (such as a concert series or sports tournament); an activity of extended or indefinite duration (such as an art exhibit); or continuing support of an exempt organization's operation. See Prop. Treas. Reg. § 1.513-4(f); Preamble to Proposed Regulations on Corporate Sponsorship, REG 209601-92, reprinted in 28 Exempt Org. Tax Rev. 133 (2000). The 1993 proposed regulations were somewhat more restrictive, suggesting that a QSP must be linked to a single event.

(2) A payment may be a QSP even if the sponsored activity conducted by the organization is not substantially related to its exempt purposes. Prop. Treas. Reg. § 1.513-4(f).

(3) Although § 513(i) removes the "tainting" rule (see casebook, p. 797), an exempt organization seeking to come within the QSP safe harbor still must establish that some portion of a payment exceeds the fair market value of any substantial return benefit received by a payor in return for making the payment. The proposed regulations place the burden of establishing the fair market value of any substantial return benefit on the exempt organization, and they provide that the organization's valuation

will be accepted if it is reasonable and made in good faith. Prop. Treas. Reg. § 1.513-4(d).

(4) The right to be an exclusive sponsor of an activity (without any advertising or other substantial return benefit to the payor) -- such as for a museum exhibit or bowl game with a single corporate sponsor -- is generally not considered to be a substantial return benefit. But an exclusive *provider* agreement -- such as where, in return for a payment, an exempt organization agrees that products or services that compete with the payor's products or services will not be sold in connection with one or more of the exempt organization's activities -- are not within the QSP safe harbor. Prop. Treas. Reg. § 1.513-4(c)(2)(v). If a payor receives both exclusive sponsorship and exclusive provider rights in exchange for making a payment, the fair market value of the exclusive provider arrangement and any other substantial return benefit is determined first in making the required allocation between taxable and excluded payments. Prop. Treas. Reg. § 1.513-4(f) Example 6.

(5) When an exempt organization conducts both an unrelated business activity and an exempt activity, the proposed regulations are not as permissive as the 1993 version in allowing excess expenses from the exempt activity to be deducted against income from the taxable activity. Under the proposed regulations, excess expenses from an exempt activity are deductible only if that activity is closely connected to the unrelated business such that a taxable activity pursuing the same business normally also would conduct the exempt activity. For example, a net loss related to a museum's publication of an exhibition catalog may be applied to offset any net unrelated business income from the museum's sale of advertising in the catalog because sale of advertising "exploits" an activity -- the publication of editorial material -- normally conducted by taxable entities that sell advertising. But net expenses of the exhibition itself are treated as not sufficiently connected and thus may not be deducted against income from the advertising activity. Prop. Reg. § 1.512(a)-1(e) Example 2.

(6) Qualified sponsorship payments in the form of money or property (but not services) qualify as public support in determining whether an organization qualifies as a public charity and thus avoids private foundation status under §§ 170(b)(1)(A)(vi) or 509(a)(2). See casebook, pp. 646, 648-649.

The most controversial position in the proposed regulations is the treatment of exclusive provider agreements. Assume, for example, the increasingly common situation where a university receives a substantial payment from a soft drink company or athletic gear manufacturer and agrees in return that only that company's products may be sold on campus. Under the proposed regulations, the payment would not come within the QSP safe harbor, but query whether that resolves the question of whether the payment is taxable under general UBIT principles.

The proposed regulations do not address any issues arising from the use of the Internet by exempt organizations. The IRS is engaged in an ongoing review of the Internet activities of nonprofits, and it has specifically requested advice on the applicability of rules governing periodicals and trade shows in § 513(i)(2)(B)(ii) to an exempt organization's Internet site and how to apply the UBIT advertising rules when an exempt organization receives payments for placing banners (e.g., with a sponsor's name or logo) or electronic links to a for-profit company's web site. See I.R.S. Ann. 2000-82, 2000-42 I.R.B. 385.

C. EXCLUSIONS FROM UNRELATED BUSINESS TAXABLE INCOME

3. ROYALTIES

Page 814:

After the second full paragraph, insert:

After losing virtually every recent case, the IRS National Office has issued an order to stop litigating affinity card and mailing list cases, at least where the exempt organization does not perform any significant marketing or administrative services. See Fred Stokeld, IRS Memo Tells Area Managers to Stop Litigating Affinity Card, Mailing List Cases, 28 Exempt Org. Tax Rev. 18 (2000).

CHAPTER 9

CHARITABLE CONTRIBUTIONS

B. CHARITABLE CONTRIBUTIONS: BASIC PRINCIPLES

6. EMERGING INTERNET ISSUES

Fundraising over the Internet continues to proliferate, raising a handful of tax questions along with the state law charitable solicitation issues discussed in Chapter 4 of the casebook.

Some solicitations are being made by for-profit firms on behalf of specified charitable organizations. Contributions are collected through secure connections using credit cards and the solicitor remits the gift to the charity after keeping a fee. If the solicitor is acting as the charity's agent, the full amount of the gift should be deductible, with the fee being treated as an expense of the charity. In other cases (and how is the donor to know?), the fee would not be a deductible contribution because the intermediary is the donor's agent. The legal relationship of the solicitor to the charity also may affect the timing of a deduction. If the solicitor is the donor's agent, the gift is not complete until remitted to the charity, but a deduction should be available upon a click of the mouse if the solicitor is the charity's agent.

In its request for comments in Announcement 2000-84, 2000-42 I.R.B. 385, the Service asked whether e-mail acknowledgements and disclosures of "quid pro quo" return benefits satisfied the substantiation and disclosure rules in §§ 170(f)(8) and 6115. The answer in both cases should be yes, at least if the electronic acknowledgements can be printed out and contain the required information. A related question is whether Internet solicitations (either on a web site or by e-mail) are in "written or printed form" within the meaning of I.R.C. § 6113(c)(1)(A), in which case organizations (such as § 501(c)(4) advocacy groups) that are not eligible to receive deductible gifts must include an express statement to that effect in "a conspicuous and easily recognizable format."

What about a web surfer who visits an on line "charity mall" where "commissions" paid by on-line merchants on all purchases made through the site are remitted to charities selected by the purchasers from a list. A well known charitable mall, in response to a "frequently asked question," advises donors that they may not take any tax deduction because they are buying goods and services at regular prices and not making a donation directly to the charity. See <www.charitablemall.com>. May the merchants (who don't select the donee) take the deduction? In a variation on this theme, another web-based merchant/solicitor (iGive.com) allows members to purchase products from vendors who then send back rebates which the buyer either may keep or designate to selected charities. In this situation, members are told that rebates designated to charities are tax-deductible (because the member may keep the rebate or donate it. But donations over $250 to any single cause are now allowed in any single month (why?).

For Further Reading. Christina L. Nooney, Tax-Exempt Organizations and the Internet, 27 Exempt Org. Tax Rev. 33 (2000); Catherine E. Livingston, Tax-Exempt Organizations and the Internet: Tax and Other Legal Issues, 31 Exempt Org. Tax Rev. 419 (2001).

PART FOUR

OTHER LEGAL ISSUES AFFECTING NONPROFIT ORGANIZATIONS

CHAPTER 10

SPECIAL PROBLEMS OF PRIVATE MEMBERSHIP ASSOCIATIONS

F. PRIVATE ASSOCIATIONS AND THE CONSTITUTION

1. FREEDOM OF ASSOCIATION

Page 997:

   After the second full paragraph, insert:

BOY SCOUTS OF AMERICA v. DALE

Supreme Court of the United States, 2000.
2000 WL 82694.

Chief Justice REHNQUIST delivered the opinion of the Court.

Petitioners are the Boy Scouts of America and the Monmouth Council, a division of the Boy Scouts of America (collectively, Boy Scouts). The Boy Scouts is a private, not-for-profit organization engaged in instilling its system of values in young people. The Boy Scouts asserts that homosexual conduct is inconsistent with the values it seeks to instill. Respondent is James Dale, a former Eagle Scout whose adult membership in the Boy Scouts was revoked when the Boy Scouts learned that he is an avowed homosexual and gay rights activist. The New Jersey Supreme Court held that New Jersey's public accommodations law requires that the Boy Scouts admit Dale. This case presents the question whether applying New Jersey's public accommodations law in this way violates the Boy Scouts' First Amendment right of expressive association. We hold that it does.

41

I

James Dale entered scouting in 1978 at the age of eight by joining Monmouth Council's Cub Scout Pack 142. Dale became a Boy Scout in 1981 and remained a Scout until he turned 18. By all accounts, Dale was an exemplary Scout. In 1988, he achieved the rank of Eagle Scout, one of Scouting's highest honors.

Dale applied for adult membership in the Boy Scouts in 1989. The Boy Scouts approved his application for the position of assistant scoutmaster of Troop 73. Around the same time, Dale left home to attend Rutgers University. After arriving at Rutgers, Dale first acknowledged to himself and others that he is gay. He quickly became involved with, and eventually became the copresident of, the Rutgers University Lesbian/Gay Alliance. In 1990, Dale attended a seminar addressing the psychological and health needs of lesbian and gay teenagers. A newspaper covering the event interviewed Dale about his advocacy of homosexual teenagers' need for gay role models. In early July 1990, the newspaper published the interview and Dale's photograph over a caption identifying him as the copresident of the Lesbian/Gay Alliance.

Later that month, Dale received a letter from Monmouth Council Executive James Kay revoking his adult membership. Dale wrote to Kay requesting the reason for Monmouth Council's decision. Kay responded by letter that the Boy Scouts "specifically forbid membership to homosexuals."

* * *

[The Court then traced the path of the case through the lower New Jersey courts. Eds.]

The New Jersey Supreme Court * * * held that the Boy Scouts was a place of public accommodation subject to the public accommodations law, that the organization was not exempt from the law under any of its express exceptions, and that the Boy Scouts violated the law by revoking Dale's membership based on his avowed homosexuality. After considering the state-law issues, the court addressed the Boy Scouts' claims that application of the public accommodations law in this case violated its federal constitutional rights " 'to enter into and maintain * * * intimate or private relationships * * * [and] to associate for the purpose of engaging in protected speech.' " With respect to the right to intimate association, the court concluded that the Boy Scouts' "large size, nonselectivity, inclusive rather than exclusive purpose, and practice of inviting or allowing nonmembers to attend meetings, establish that the organization is not 'sufficiently personal or private to warrant constitutional protection' under the freedom of intimate association.' " With respect to the right of expressive association, the court "agree[d] that Boy Scouts expresses a belief in moral values and uses its activities to encourage the moral development of its members." But the court concluded that it was "not persuaded ... that a shared goal of Boy Scout members is to associate in order to preserve the view that homosexuality is immoral." Accordingly, the court held "that Dale's membership does not violate the Boy Scouts' right of expressive association because his inclusion would not 'affect in any significant way [the Boy Scouts'] existing members' ability to carry out their various purposes.'" The court also determined that New Jersey has a compelling interest in eliminating "the destructive consequences of discrimination from our society," and that its public accommodations law abridges no more speech than is necessary to accomplish its purpose. Finally, the court addressed the Boy Scouts' reliance on Hurley v. Irish-American Gay, Lesbian and Bisexual Group of Boston, Inc., 515 U.S. 557, 115 S.Ct. 2338 (1995), in support of its claimed First Amendment right to exclude Dale. The court determined that Hurley did not require deciding the case in favor of the Boy Scouts because "the reinstatement of Dale does not compel Boy Scouts to express any message."

We granted the Boy Scouts' petition for certiorari to determine whether the application of New Jersey's public accommodations law violated the First Amendment.

II

In Roberts v. United States Jaycees, 468 U.S. 609, 622, 104 S.Ct. 3244 (1984), we observed that "implicit in the right to engage in activities protected by the First Amendment" is "a corresponding right to associate with others in pursuit of a wide variety of political, social, economic, educational, religious, and cultural ends." This right is crucial in preventing the majority from imposing its views on groups that would rather express other, perhaps unpopular, ideas. See ibid. (stating that protection of the right to expressive association is "especially important in preserving political and cultural diversity and in shielding dissident expression from suppression by the majority"). Government actions that may unconstitutionally burden this freedom may take many forms, one of which is "intrusion into the internal structure or affairs of an association" like a "regulation that forces the group to accept members it does not desire." Id., at 623. Forcing a group to accept certain members may impair the ability of the group to express those views, and only those views, that it intends to express. Thus, "[f] reedom of association * * * plainly presupposes a freedom not to associate."

The forced inclusion of an unwanted person in a group infringes the group's freedom of expressive association if the presence of that person affects in a significant way the group's ability to advocate public or private viewpoints. New York State Club Assn., Inc. v. City of New York, 487 U.S. 1, 13, 108 S.Ct. 2225 (1988). But the freedom of expressive association, like many freedoms, is not absolute. We have held that the freedom could be overridden "by regulations adopted to serve compelling state interests, unrelated to the suppression of ideas, that cannot be achieved through means significantly less restrictive of associational freedoms." Roberts, supra, at 623.

To determine whether a group is protected by the First Amendment's expressive associational right, we must determine whether the group engages in "expressive association." The First Amendment's protection of expressive association is not reserved for advocacy groups. But to come within its ambit, a group must engage in some form of expression, whether it be public or private.

Because this is a First Amendment case where the ultimate conclusions of law are virtually inseparable from findings of fact, we are obligated to independently review the factual record to ensure that the state court's judgment does not unlawfully intrude on free expression. The record reveals the following. The Boy Scouts is a private, nonprofit organization. According to its mission statement:

"It is the mission of the Boy Scouts of America to serve others by helping to instill values in young people and, in other ways, to prepare them to make ethical choices over their lifetime in achieving their full potential.

"The values we strive to instill are based on those found in the Scout Oath and Law:

[The Court then recited the Scout Oath[***] and Scout Law[****]. Eds.]

Thus, the general mission of the Boy Scouts is clear: "[T]o instill values in young people." The Boy Scouts seeks to instill these values by having its adult leaders spend time with the youth members, instructing and engaging them in activities like camping, archery, and fishing. During the time spent with the youth members, the scoutmasters and assistant scoutmasters inculcate them with the Boy Scouts' values--both expressly and by example. It seems indisputable that an association that seeks to transmit such a system of values engages in expressive activity. See Roberts, supra, at 636 (O'CONNOR, J., concurring) ("Even the training of outdoor survival skills or participation in community service might become expressive when the activity is intended to develop good morals, reverence, patriotism, and a desire for self- improvement").

Given that the Boy Scouts engages in expressive activity, we must determine whether the forced inclusion of Dale as an assistant scoutmaster would significantly

---

[***]"On my honor I will do my best To do my duty to God and my country and to obey the Scout Law; To help other people at all times; To keep myself physically strong, mentally awake, and morally straight."

[****]"A Scout is: "Trustworthy Obedient Loyal Cheerful Helpful Thrifty Friendly Brave Courteous Clean Kind Reverent."

affect the Boy Scouts' ability to advocate public or private viewpoints. This inquiry necessarily requires us first to explore, to a limited extent, the nature of the Boy Scouts' view of homosexuality.

The values the Boy Scouts seeks to instill are "based on" those listed in the Scout Oath and Law. The Boy Scouts explains that the Scout Oath and Law provide "a positive moral code for living; they are a list of 'do's' rather than 'don'ts.'" The Boy Scouts asserts that homosexual conduct is inconsistent with the values embodied in the Scout Oath and Law, particularly with the values represented by the terms "morally straight" and "clean."

Obviously, the Scout Oath and Law do not expressly mention sexuality or sexual orientation. And the terms "morally straight" and "clean" are by no means self-defining. Different people would attribute to those terms very different meanings. For example, some people may believe that engaging in homosexual conduct is not at odds with being "morally straight" and "clean." And others may believe that engaging in homosexual conduct is contrary to being "morally straight" and "clean." The Boy Scouts says it falls within the latter category.

The New Jersey Supreme Court analyzed the Boy Scouts' beliefs and found that the "exclusion of members solely on the basis of their sexual orientation is inconsistent with Boy Scouts' commitment to a diverse and 'representative' membership * * * [and] contradicts Boy Scouts' overarching objective to reach 'all eligible youth.'" The court concluded that the exclusion of members like Dale "appears antithetical to the organization's goals and philosophy." But our cases reject this sort of inquiry; it is not the role of the courts to reject a group's expressed values because they disagree with those values or find them internally inconsistent.

The Boy Scouts asserts that it "teach[es] that homosexual conduct is not morally straight," and that it does "not want to promote homosexual conduct as a legitimate form of behavior." We accept the Boy Scouts' assertion. We need not inquire further to determine the nature of the Boy Scouts' expression with respect to homosexuality. But because the record before us contains written evidence of the Boy Scouts' viewpoint, we look to it as instructive, if only on the question of the sincerity of the professed beliefs.

A 1978 position statement to the Boy Scouts' Executive Committee, signed by Downing B. Jenks, the President of the Boy Scouts, and Harvey L. Price, the Chief Scout Executive, expresses the Boy Scouts' "official position" with regard to "homosexuality and Scouting":

"Q. May an individual who openly declares himself to be a homosexual be a volunteer Scout leader?

"A. No. The Boy Scouts of America is a private, membership organization and leadership therein is a privilege and not a right. We do not believe that homosexuality and leadership in Scouting are appropriate. We will continue to select only those who in our judgment meet our standards and qualifications for leadership."

Thus, at least as of 1978--the year James Dale entered Scouting--the official position of the Boy Scouts was that avowed homosexuals were not to be Scout leaders.

A position statement promulgated by the Boy Scouts in 1991 (after Dale's membership was revoked but before this litigation was filed) also supports its current view:

"We believe that homosexual conduct is inconsistent with the requirement in the Scout Oath that a Scout be morally straight and in the Scout Law that a Scout be clean in word and deed, and that homosexuals do not provide a desirable role model for Scouts."

This position statement was redrafted numerous times but its core message remained consistent. For example, a 1993 position statement, the most recent in the record, reads, in part:

"The Boy Scouts of America has always reflected the expectations that Scouting families have had for the organization. We do not believe that homosexuals provide a role model consistent with these expectations. Accordingly, we do not allow for the registration of avowed homosexuals as members or as leaders of the BSA."

The Boy Scouts publicly expressed its views with respect to homosexual conduct by its assertions in prior litigation. * * * We cannot doubt that the Boy Scouts sincerely holds this view.

We must then determine whether Dale's presence as an assistant scoutmaster would significantly burden the Boy Scouts' desire to not "promote homosexual conduct as a legitimate form of behavior." As we give deference to an association's assertions regarding the nature of its expression, we must also give deference to an association's view of what would impair its expression. That is not to say that an expressive association can erect a shield against antidiscrimination laws simply by asserting that mere acceptance of a member from a particular group would impair its message. But here Dale, by his own admission, is one of a group of gay Scouts who have "become leaders in their community and are open and honest about their sexual orientation." Dale was the copresident of a gay and lesbian organization at college and remains a gay rights activist. Dale's presence in the Boy Scouts would, at the very least, force the organization to send a message, both to the youth members and the world, that the Boy Scouts accepts homosexual conduct as a legitimate form of behavior.

Hurley is illustrative on this point. There we considered whether the application of Massachusetts' public accommodations law to require the organizers of a private St. Patrick's Day parade to include among the marchers an Irish-American gay, lesbian, and bisexual group, GLIB, violated the parade organizers' First Amendment rights. We noted that the parade organizers did not wish to exclude the GLIB members because of their sexual orientations, but because they wanted to march behind a GLIB banner. We observed:

> "[A] contingent marching behind the organization's banner would at least bear witness to the fact that some Irish are gay, lesbian, or bisexual, and the presence of the organized marchers would suggest their view that people of their sexual orientations have as much claim to unqualified social acceptance as heterosexuals. * * * The parade's organizers may not believe these facts about Irish sexuality to be so, or they may object to unqualified social acceptance of gays and lesbians or have some other reason for wishing to keep GLIB's message out of the parade. But whatever the reason, it boils down to the choice of a speaker not to propound a particular point of view, and that choice is presumed to lie beyond the government's power to control."

Here, we have found that the Boy Scouts believes that homosexual conduct is inconsistent with the values it seeks to instill in its youth members; it will not "promote homosexual conduct as a legitimate form of behavior." As the presence of GLIB in Boston's St. Patrick's Day parade would have interfered with the parade organizers' choice not to propound a particular point of view, the presence of Dale as an assistant scoutmaster would just as surely interfere with the Boy Scout's choice not to propound a point of view contrary to its beliefs.

The New Jersey Supreme Court determined that the Boy Scouts' ability to disseminate its message was not significantly affected by the forced inclusion of Dale as an assistant scoutmaster because of the following findings:

> "Boy Scout members do not associate for the purpose of disseminating the belief that homosexuality is immoral; Boy Scouts discourages its leaders from disseminating any views on sexual issues; and Boy Scouts includes sponsors and members who subscribe to different views in respect of homosexuality."

We disagree with the New Jersey Supreme Court's conclusion drawn from these findings.

First, associations do not have to associate for the "purpose" of disseminating a certain message in order to be entitled to the protections of the First Amendment.

An association must merely engage in expressive activity that could be impaired in order to be entitled to protection. For example, the purpose of the St. Patrick's Day parade in Hurley was not to espouse any views about sexual orientation, but we held that the parade organizers had a right to exclude certain participants nonetheless.

Second, even if the Boy Scouts discourages Scout leaders from disseminating views on sexual issues--a fact that the Boy Scouts disputes with contrary evidence--the First Amendment protects the Boy Scouts' method of expression. If the Boy Scouts wishes Scout leaders to avoid questions of sexuality and teach only by example, this fact does not negate the sincerity of its belief discussed above.

Third, the First Amendment simply does not require that every member of a group agree on every issue in order for the group's policy to be "expressive association." The Boy Scouts takes an official position with respect to homosexual conduct, and that is sufficient for First Amendment purposes. In this same vein, Dale makes much of the claim that the Boy Scouts does not revoke the membership of heterosexual Scout leaders that openly disagree with the Boy Scouts' policy on sexual orientation. But if this is true, it is irrelevant. The presence of an avowed homosexual and gay rights activist in an assistant scoutmaster's uniform sends a distinctly different message from the presence of a heterosexual assistant scoutmaster who is on record as disagreeing with Boy Scouts policy. The Boy Scouts has a First Amendment right to choose to send one message but not the other. The fact that the organization does not trumpet its views from the housetops, or that it tolerates dissent within its ranks, does not mean that its views receive no First Amendment protection.

Having determined that the Boy Scouts is an expressive association and that the forced inclusion of Dale would significantly affect its expression, we inquire whether the application of New Jersey's public accommodations law to require that the Boy Scouts accept Dale as an assistant scoutmaster runs afoul of the Scouts' freedom of expressive association. We conclude that it does.

State public accommodations laws were originally enacted to prevent discrimination in traditional places of public accommodation--like inns and trains. Over time, the public accommodations laws have expanded to cover more places. New Jersey's statutory definition of "'[a] place of public accommodation'" is extremely broad. The term is said to "include, but not be limited to," a list of over 50 types of places. Many on the list are what one would expect to be places where the public is invited. For example, the statute includes as places of public accommodation taverns, restaurants, retail shops, and public libraries. But the statute also includes places that often may not carry with them open invitations to the public, like summer camps and roof gardens. In this case, the New Jersey Supreme Court went a step further and applied its public accommodations law to a private entity without even attempting to tie the term "place" to a physical location. As the definition of "public accommodation" has expanded from clearly commercial entities, such as restaurants, bars, and hotels, to membership organizations such as the Boy Scouts, the potential for conflict between state public accommodations laws and the First Amendment rights of organizations has increased.

We recognized in cases such as Roberts and Duarte that States have a compelling interest in eliminating discrimination against women in public accommodations. But in each of these cases we went on to conclude that the enforcement of these statutes would not materially interfere with the ideas that the organization sought to express. *** We thereupon concluded in each of these cases that the organizations' First Amendment rights were not violated by the application of the States' public accommodations laws.

In Hurley, we said that public accommodations laws "are well within the State's usual power to enact when a legislature has reason to believe that a given group is the target of discrimination, and they do not, as a general matter, violate the First or Fourteenth Amendments." But we went on to note that in that case "the Massachusetts [public accommodations] law has been applied in a peculiar way" because "any contingent of protected individuals with a message would have the right to participate in petitioners' speech, so that the communication produced by the private organizers would be shaped by all those protected by the law who wish to join in with some expressive demonstration of their own." And in the associational freedom cases such as Roberts, Duarte, and New York State Club Assn., after finding a compelling state interest, the Court went on to examine whether or not the application of the state law would impose any "serious burden" on the organization's rights of expressive association. So in these cases, the associational interest in freedom of expression has been set on one side of the scale, and the State's interest on the other.

* * *

We have already concluded that a state requirement that the Boy Scouts retain Dale as an assistant scoutmaster would significantly burden the organization's right to oppose or disfavor homosexual conduct. The state interests embodied in New Jersey's public accommodations law do not justify such a severe intrusion on the Boy Scouts' rights to freedom of expressive association. That being the case, we hold that the First Amendment prohibits the State from imposing such a requirement through the application of its public accommodations law.

JUSTICE STEVENS' dissent makes much of its observation that the public perception of homosexuality in this country has changed. Indeed, it appears that homosexuality has gained greater societal acceptance. But this is scarcely an argument for denying First Amendment protection to those who refuse to accept these views. The First Amendment protects expression, be it of the popular variety or not. And the fact that an idea may be embraced and advocated by increasing numbers of people is all the more reason to protect the First Amendment rights of those who wish to voice a different view.

* * *

We are not, as we must not be, guided by our views of whether the Boy Scouts' teachings with respect to homosexual conduct are right or wrong; public or judicial disapproval of a tenet of an organization's expression does not justify the State's effort to compel the organization to accept members where such acceptance would derogate from the organization's expressive message. "While the law is free to promote all sorts of conduct in place of harmful behavior, it is not free to interfere with speech for no better reason than promoting an approved message or discouraging a disfavored one, however enlightened either purpose may strike the government."

The judgment of the New Jersey Supreme Court is reversed, and the cause remanded for further proceedings not inconsistent with this opinion.

It is so ordered.

[The Appendix to the opinion of the Court is omitted. Eds.]

JUSTICE STEVENS, with whom JUSTICE SOUTER, JUSTICE GINSBURG and JUSTICE BREYER join, dissenting.

New Jersey "prides itself on judging each individual by his or her merits" and on being "in the vanguard in the fight to eradicate the cancer of unlawful discrimination of all types from our society." Since 1945, it has had a law against discrimination. The law broadly protects the opportunity of all persons to obtain the advantages and privileges "of any place of public accommodation." The New Jersey Supreme Court's construction of the statutory definition of a "place of public accommodation" has given its statute a more expansive coverage than most similar state statutes. And as amended in 1991, the law prohibits discrimination on the basis of nine different traits including an individual's "sexual orientation." The question in this case is whether that expansive construction trenches on the federal constitutional rights of the Boy Scouts of America (BSA).

* * *

The majority holds that New Jersey's law violates BSA's right to associate and its right to free speech. But that law does not "impos[e] any serious burdens" on BSA's "collective effort on behalf of [its] shared goals," nor does it force BSA to communicate any message that it does not wish to endorse. New Jersey's law, therefore, abridges no constitutional right of the Boy Scouts.

I

* * *

In this case, Boy Scouts of America contends that it teaches the young boys who are Scouts that homosexuality is immoral. Consequently, it argues, it would violate its right to associate to force it to admit homosexuals as members, as doing so would be at odds with its own shared goals and values. This contention, quite plainly, requires us to look at what, exactly, are the values that BSA actually teaches.

* * *

[Justice Stevens then examined the Boy Scouts' Statement of Mission as expressed through its publications. Eds.]

It is plain as the light of day that neither one of these principles--"morally straight" and "clean"--says the slightest thing about homosexuality. Indeed, neither term in the Boy Scouts' Law and Oath expresses any position whatsoever on sexual matters.

BSA's published guidance on that topic underscores this point. Scouts, for example, are directed to receive their sex education at home or in school, but not from the organization: "Your parents or guardian or a sex education teacher should give you the facts about sex that you must know." Boy Scout Handbook (1992) To be sure, Scouts are not forbidden from asking their Scoutmaster about issues of a sexual nature, but Scoutmasters are, literally, the last person Scouts are encouraged to ask: "If you have questions about growing up, about relationships, sex, or making good decisions, ask. Talk with your parents, religious leaders, teachers, or Scoutmaster." Ibid. Moreover, Scoutmasters are specifically directed to steer curious adolescents to other sources of information[.] "If Scouts ask for information regarding * * * sexual activity, answer honestly and factually, but stay within your realm of expertise and comfort. If a Scout has serious concerns that you cannot answer, refer him to his family, religious leader, doctor, or other professional." Scoutmaster Handbook (1990). More specifically, BSA has set forth a number of rules for Scoutmasters when these types of issues come up: "You may have boys asking you for information or advice about sexual matters. * * * "How should you handle such matters? "Rule number 1: You do not undertake to instruct Scouts, in any formalized manner, in the subject of sex and family life. The reasons are that it is not construed to be Scouting's proper area, and that you are probably not well qualified to do this. "Rule number 2: If Scouts come to you to ask questions or to seek advice, you would give it within your competence. A boy who appears to be asking about sexual intercourse, however, may really only be worried about his pimples, so it is well to find out just what information is needed. "Rule number 3: You should refer boys with sexual problems to persons better qualified than you [are] to handle them. If the boy has a spiritual leader or a doctor who can deal with them, he should go there. If such persons are not available, you may just have to do the best you can. But don't try to play a highly professional role. And at the other extreme, avoid passing the buck."

In light of BSA's self-proclaimed ecumenism, furthermore, it is even more difficult to discern any shared goals or common moral stance on homosexuality. Insofar as religious matters are concerned, BSA's bylaws state that it is "absolutely nonsectarian in its attitude toward * * * religious training."

II

The Court seeks to fill the void by pointing to a statement of "policies and procedures relating to homosexuality and Scouting" signed by BSA's President and Chief Scout Executive in 1978 and addressed to the members of the Executive Committee of the national organization. The letter says that the BSA does "not believe that homosexuality and leadership in Scouting are appropriate." * * *

Four aspects of the 1978 policy statement are relevant to the proper disposition of this case. First, at most this letter simply adopts an exclusionary membership policy. But simply adopting such a policy has never been considered sufficient, by itself, to prevail on a right to associate claim.

Second, the 1978 policy was never publicly expressed--unlike, for example, the Scout's duty to be "obedient." It was an internal memorandum, never circulated beyond the few members of BSA's Executive Committee. It remained, in effect, a secret Boy Scouts policy. Far from claiming any intent to express an idea that would be burdened by the presence of homosexuals, BSA's public posture--to the world and to the Scouts themselves--remained what it had always been: one of tolerance, welcoming all classes of boys and young men. In this respect, BSA's claim is even weaker than those we have rejected in the past.

Third, it is apparent that the draftsmen of the policy statement foresaw the possibility that laws against discrimination might one day be amended to protect homosexuals from employment discrimination. Their statement clearly provided that, in the event such a law conflicted with their policy, a Scout's duty to be "obedient" and "obe[y] the laws," even if "he thinks [the laws] are unfair" would prevail in such a contingency. In 1978, however, BSA apparently did not consider it to be a serious possibility that a State might one day characterize the Scouts as a "place of public accommodation" with a duty to open its membership to all qualified individuals. The portions of the statement dealing with membership simply assume that membership in the Scouts is a "privilege" that BSA is free to grant or to withhold. The statement does not address the question whether the publicly proclaimed duty to obey the law should prevail over the private discriminatory policy if, and when, a conflict between the two should arise--as it now has in New Jersey. At the very least, then, the statement reflects no unequivocal view on homosexuality. Indeed, the statement suggests that an appropriate way for BSA to preserve its unpublished exclusionary policy would include an open and forthright attempt to seek an amendment of New Jersey's statute. ("If he thinks these rules and laws are unfair, he tries to have them changed in an orderly manner rather than disobey them.")

Fourth, the 1978 statement simply says that homosexuality is not "appropriate." It makes no effort to connect that statement to a shared goal or expressive activity of the Boy Scouts. Whatever values BSA seeks to instill in Scouts, the idea that homosexuality is not "appropriate" appears entirely unconnected to, and is mentioned nowhere in, the myriad of publicly declared values and creeds of the BSA. That idea does not appear to be among any of the principles actually taught to Scouts. Rather, the 1978 policy appears to be no more than a private statement of a few BSA executives that the organization wishes to exclude gays--and that wish has nothing to do with any expression BSA actually engages in.

The majority also relies on four other policy statements that were issued between 1991 and 1993. All of them were written and issued after BSA revoked Dale's membership. Accordingly, they have little, if any, relevance to the legal question before this Court. In any event, they do not bolster BSA's claim.

* * *

It is clear, then, that nothing in these policy statements supports BSA's claim. The only policy written before the revocation of Dale's membership was an equivocal, undisclosed statement that evidences no connection between the group's discriminatory intentions and its expressive interests. The later policies demonstrate a brief--though ultimately abandoned--attempt to tie BSA's exclusion to its expression, but other than a single sentence, BSA fails to show that it ever taught Scouts that homosexuality is not "morally straight" or "clean," or that such a view was part of the group's collective efforts to foster a belief. Furthermore, BSA's policy statements fail to establish any clear, consistent, and unequivocal position on homosexuality. Nor did BSA have any reason to think Dale's sexual conduct, as opposed to his orientation, was contrary to the group's values.

BSA's inability to make its position clear and its failure to connect its alleged policy to its expressive activities is highly significant. By the time Dale was expelled from the Boy Scouts in 1990, BSA had already been engaged in several suits under a variety of state antidiscrimination public accommodation laws challenging various aspects of its membership policy. * * * [I]t was clearly on notice by 1990 that it might well be subjected to state public accommodation antidiscrimination laws, and that a court might one day reject its claimed right to associate. Yet it took no steps prior to Dale's expulsion to clarify how its exclusivity was connected to its expression. It speaks volumes about the credibility of BSA's claim to a shared goal that homosexuality is incompatible with Scouting that since at least 1984 it had been aware of this issue--indeed, concerned enough to twice file amicus briefs before this Court--yet it did nothing in the intervening six years (or even in the years after Dale's expulsion) to explain clearly and openly why the presence of homosexuals would affect its expressive activities, or to make the view of "morally straight" and "clean" taken in its 1991 and 1992 policies a part of the values actually instilled in Scouts through the Handbook, lessons, or otherwise.

III

BSA's claim finds no support in our cases. We have recognized "a right to associate for the purpose of engaging in those activities protected by the First Amendment--speech, assembly, petition for the redress of grievances, and the exercise of religion." Roberts, 468 U.S., at 618. And we have acknowledged that "when the State interferes with individuals' selection of those with whom they wish to join in a common endeavor, freedom of association * * * may be implicated." Ibid. But "[t]he right to associate for expressive purposes is not * * * absolute"; rather, "the nature and degree of constitutional protection afforded freedom of association may vary depending on the extent to which * * * the constitutionally protected liberty is at stake in a given case." Indeed, the right to associate does not mean "that in every setting in which individuals exercise some discrimination in choosing associates, their selective process of inclusion and exclusion is protected by the Constitution." New York State Club Assn., Inc. v. City of New York, 487 U.S. 1, 13, 108 S.Ct. 2225, (1988). For example, we have routinely and easily rejected assertions of this right by expressive organizations with discriminatory membership policies, such as private schools, law firms, and labor organizations. In fact, until today, we have never once found a claimed right to associate in the selection of members to prevail in the face of a State's antidiscrimination law. To the contrary, we have squarely held that a State's antidiscrimination law does not violate a group's right to associate simply because the law conflicts with that group's exclusionary membership policy.

* * *

Several principles are made perfectly clear by Jaycees and Rotary Club. First, to prevail on a claim of expressive association in the face of a State's antidiscrimination law, it is not enough simply to engage in some kind of expressive activity. Both the Jaycees and the Rotary Club engaged in expressive activity protected by the First Amendment, yet that fact was not dispositive. Second, it is not enough to adopt an openly avowed exclusionary membership policy. Both the Jaycees and the Rotary Club did that as well. Third, it is not sufficient merely to articulate some connection between the group's expressive activities and its exclusionary policy.

* * *

The relevant question is whether the mere inclusion of the person at issue would "impose any serious burden," "affect in any significant way," or be "a substantial restraint upon" the organization's "shared goals," "basic goals," or "collective effort to foster beliefs." Accordingly, it is necessary to examine what, exactly, are BSA's shared goals and the degree to which its expressive activities would be burdened, affected, or restrained by including homosexuals.

The evidence before this Court makes it exceptionally clear that BSA has, at most, simply adopted an exclusionary membership policy and has no shared goal of disapproving of homosexuality. BSA's mission statement and federal charter say nothing on the matter; its official membership policy is silent; its Scout Oath and Law--and accompanying definitions--are devoid of any view on the topic; its guidance for Scouts and Scoutmasters on sexuality declare that such matters are "not construed to be Scouting's proper area," but are the province of a Scout's parents and pastor; and BSA's posture respecting religion tolerates a wide variety of views on the issue of homosexuality. Moreover, there is simply no evidence that BSA otherwise teaches anything in this area, or that it instructs Scouts on matters involving homosexuality in ways not conveyed in the Boy Scout or Scoutmaster Handbooks. In short, Boy Scouts of America is simply silent on homosexuality. There is no shared goal or collective effort to foster a belief about homosexuality at all--let alone one that is significantly burdened by admitting homosexuals.

As in Jaycees, there is "no basis in the record for concluding that admission of [homosexuals] will impede the [Boy Scouts'] ability to engage in [its] protected activities or to disseminate its preferred views" and New Jersey's law "requires no change in [BSA's] creed." And like Rotary Club, New Jersey's law "does not require [BSA] to abandon or alter any of" its activities. The evidence relied on by the Court is not to the contrary. The undisclosed 1978 policy certainly adds nothing to the actual views disseminated to the Scouts. It simply says that homosexuality is not "appropriate." There is no reason to give that policy statement more weight than Rotary International's assertion that all-male membership fosters the group's "fellowship" and was the only way it could "operate effectively." As for BSA's post-revocation statements, at most they simply adopt a policy of discrimination, which is no more dispositive than the openly discriminatory policies held insufficient in Jaycees and Rotary Club; there is no evidence here that BSA's policy was necessary to--or even a part of--BSA's expressive activities or was every taught to Scouts.

Equally important is BSA's failure to adopt any clear position on homosexuality. BSA's temporary, though ultimately abandoned, view that homosexuality is incompatible with being "morally straight" and "clean" is a far cry from the clear, unequivocal statement necessary to prevail on its claim. Despite the solitary sentences in the 1991 and 1992 policies, the group continued to disclaim any single religious or moral position as a general matter and actively eschewed teaching any lesson on sexuality. It also continued to define "morally straight" and "clean" in the Boy Scout and Scoutmaster Handbooks without any reference to homosexuality. As noted earlier, nothing in our cases suggests that a group can prevail on a right to expressive association if it, effectively, speaks out of both sides of its mouth. A State's antidiscrimination law does not impose a "serious burden" or a "substantial restraint" upon the group's "shared goals" if the group itself is unable to identify its own stance with any clarity.

IV

The majority pretermits this entire analysis. It finds that BSA in fact " 'teach[es] that homosexual conduct is not morally straight.' " This conclusion, remarkably, rests entirely on statements in BSA's briefs. Moreover, the majority insists that we must "give deference to an association's assertions regarding the nature of its expression" and "we must also give deference to an association's view of what would impair its expression." So long as the record "contains written evidence" to support a group's bare assertion, "[w]e need not inquire further." Once the organization "asserts" that it engages in particular expression, "[w]e cannot doubt" the truth of that assertion.

This is an astounding view of the law. I am unaware of any previous instance in which our analysis of the scope of a constitutional right was determined by looking at what a litigant asserts in his or her brief and inquiring no further. It is even more astonishing in the First Amendment area, because, as the majority itself acknowledges, "we are obligated to independently review the factual record." It is an odd form of independent review that consists of deferring entirely to whatever a litigant claims. But the majority insists that our inquiry must be "limited," because "it is not the role of the courts to reject a group's expressed values because they disagree with those values or find them internally inconsistent."

But nothing in our cases calls for this Court to do any such thing. An organization can adopt the message of its choice, and it is not this Court's place to disagree with it. But we must inquire whether the group is, in fact, expressing a message (whatever it may be) and whether that message (if one is expressed) is significantly affected by a State's antidiscrimination law. More critically, that inquiry requires our independent analysis, rather than deference to a group's litigating posture. Reflection on the subject dictates that such an inquiry is required.

Surely there are instances in which an organization that truly aims to foster a belief at odds with the purposes of a State's antidiscrimination laws will have a First Amendment right to association that precludes forced compliance with those laws. But that right is not a freedom to discriminate at will, nor is it a right to maintain an exclusionary membership policy simply out of fear of what the public reaction would be if the group's membership were opened up. It is an implicit right designed to protect the enumerated rights of the First Amendment, not a license to act on any discriminatory impulse. To prevail in asserting a right of expressive association as a defense to a charge of violating an antidiscrimination law, the organization must at least show it has adopted and advocated an unequivocal position inconsistent with a position advocated or epitomized by the person whom the organization seeks to exclude. If this Court were to defer to whatever position an organization is prepared to assert in its briefs, there would be no way to mark the proper boundary between genuine exercises of the right to associate, on the one hand, and sham claims that are simply attempts to insulate nonexpressive private discrimination, on the other hand. Shielding a litigant's claim from judicial scrutiny would, in turn, render civil rights legislation a nullity, and turn this important constitutional right into a farce. Accordingly, the Court's prescription of total deference will not do. * * *

V

* * *

The majority, though, does not rest its conclusion on the claim that Dale will use his position as a bully pulpit. Rather, it contends that Dale's mere presence among the Boy Scouts will itself force the group to convey a message about homosexuality--even if Dale has no intention of doing so. The majority holds that "[t]he presence of an avowed homosexual and gay rights activist in an assistant scoutmaster's uniform sends a distinc[t] * * * message," and, accordingly, BSA is entitled to exclude that message. In particular, "Dale's presence in the Boy Scouts would, at the very least, force the organization to send a message, both to the youth members and the world, that the Boy Scouts accepts homosexual conduct as a legitimate form of behavior."

The majority's argument relies exclusively on Hurley v. Irish-American Gay, Lesbian and Bisexual Group of Boston, Inc. * * * Though Hurley has a superficial similarity to the present case, a close inspection reveals a wide gulf between that case and the one before us today.

First, it was critical to our analysis that GLIB was actually conveying a message by participating in the parade--otherwise, the parade organizers could hardly claim that they were being forced to include any unwanted message at all. Our conclusion that GLIB was conveying a message was inextricably tied to the fact that GLIB wanted to march in a parade, as well as the manner in which it intended to march. We noted the "inherent expressiveness of marching [in a parade] to make a point," and in particular that GLIB was formed for the purpose of making a particular point about gay pride. * * *

Second, we found it relevant that GLIB's message "would likely be perceived" as the parade organizers' own speech. * * *

Dale's inclusion in the Boy Scouts is nothing like the case in Hurley. His participation sends no cognizable message to the Scouts or to the world. Unlike GLIB, Dale did not carry a banner or a sign; he did not distribute any fact sheet; and he expressed no intent to send any message. If there is any kind of message being sent, then, it is by the mere act of joining the Boy Scouts. Such an act does not constitute an instance of symbolic speech under the First Amendment.

It is true, of course, that some acts are so imbued with symbolic meaning that they qualify as "speech" under the First Amendment. At the same time, however, "[w]e cannot accept the view that an apparently limitless variety of conduct can be labeled 'speech' whenever the person engaging in the conduct intends thereby to express an idea." Though participating in the Scouts could itself conceivably send a message on some level, it is not the kind of act that we have recognized as speech. Indeed, if merely joining a group did constitute symbolic speech; and such speech were attributable to the group being joined; and that group has the right to exclude that speech (and hence, the right to exclude that person from joining), then the right of free speech effectively becomes a limitless right to exclude for every organization, whether or not it engages in any expressive activities. That cannot be, and never has been, the law.

The only apparent explanation for the majority's holding, then, is that homosexuals are simply so different from the rest of society that their presence alone--unlike any other individual's--should be singled out for special First Amendment treatment. Under the majority's reasoning, an openly gay male is irreversibly affixed with the label "homosexual." That label, even though unseen, communicates a message that permits his exclusion wherever he goes. His openness is the sole and sufficient justification for his ostracism. Though unintended, reliance on such a justification is tantamount to a constitutionally prescribed symbol of inferiority. * * *

[It] is not likely that BSA would be understood to send any message, either to Scouts or to the world, simply by admitting someone as a member. Over the years, BSA has generously welcomed over 87 million young Americans into its ranks. In 1992 over one million adults were active BSA members. The notion that an organization of that size and enormous prestige implicitly endorses the views that each of those adults may express in a non-Scouting context is simply mind boggling. Indeed, in this case there is no evidence that the young Scouts in Dale's troop, or members of their families, were even aware of his sexual orientation, either before or after his public statements at Rutgers University. It is equally farfetched to assert that Dale's open declaration of his homosexuality, reported in a local newspaper, will effectively force BSA to send a message to anyone simply because it allows Dale to be an Assistant Scoutmaster. For an Olympic gold medal winner or a Wimbledon tennis champion, being "openly gay" perhaps communicates a message--for example, that openness about one's sexual orientation is more virtuous than concealment; that a homosexual person can be a capable and virtuous person who should be judged like anyone else; and that homosexuality is not immoral--but it certainly does not follow that they necessarily send a message on behalf of the organizations that sponsor the activities in which they excel. The fact that such persons participate in these organizations is not usually construed to convey a message on behalf of those organizations any more than does the inclusion of women, African-Americans, religious minorities, or any other discrete group. Surely the organizations are not forced by antidiscrimination laws to take any position on the legitimacy of any individual's private beliefs or private conduct.

The State of New Jersey has decided that people who are open and frank about their sexual orientation are entitled to equal access to employment as school teachers, police officers, librarians, athletic coaches, and a host of other jobs filled by citizens who serve as role models for children and adults alike. Dozens of Scout units throughout the State are sponsored by public agencies, such as schools and fire departments, that employ such role models. BSA's affiliation with numerous public agencies that comply with New Jersey's law against discrimination cannot be understood to convey any particular message endorsing or condoning the activities of all these people.

VI

Unfavorable opinions about homosexuals "have ancient roots." Over the years, however, interaction with real people, rather than mere adherence to traditional ways of thinking about members of unfamiliar classes, have modified those opinions. A few examples: The American Psychiatric Association's and the American Psychological Association's removal of "homosexuality" from their lists of mental disorders; a move toward greater understanding within some religious communities; Justice Blackmun's classic opinion in Bowers; Georgia's invalidation of the statute upheld in Bowers; and New Jersey's enactment of the provision at issue in this case. * * *

That such prejudices are still prevalent and that they have caused serious and tangible harm to countless members of the class New Jersey seeks to protect are established matters of fact that neither the Boy Scouts nor the Court disputes. That harm can only be aggravated by the creation of a constitutional shield for a policy that is itself the product of a habitual way of thinking about strangers. As Justice

Brandeis so wisely advised, "we must be ever on our guard, lest we erect our prejudices into legal principles."

If we would guide by the light of reason, we must let our minds be bold. I respectfully dissent.

[The decision of Mr Justice Souter with whom Justices Ginsburg and Breyer join, dissenting, is omitted. Eds.]

STATUTES AND REGULATIONS APPENDIX

THE VOLUNTEER PROTECTION ACT OF 1997
(42 U.S.C. 14501-14505)

UNITED STATES CODE ANNOTATED
TITLE 42. THE PUBLIC HEALTH AND WELFARE
CHAPTER 139--VOLUNTEER PROTECTION

§ 14501. Findings and purpose

(a) Findings

The Congress finds and declares that--

(1) the willingness of volunteers to offer their services is deterred by the potential for liability actions against them;

(2) as a result, many nonprofit public and private organizations and governmental entities, including voluntary associations, social service agencies, educational institutions, and other civic programs, have been adversely affected by the withdrawal of volunteers from boards of directors and service in other capacities;

(3) the contribution of these programs to their communities is thereby diminished, resulting in fewer and higher cost programs than would be obtainable if volunteers were participating;

(4) because Federal funds are expended on useful and cost-effective social service programs, many of which are national in scope, depend heavily on volunteer participation, and represent some of the most successful public-private partnerships, protection of volunteerism through clarification and limitation of the personal liability risks assumed by the volunteer in connection with such participation is an appropriate subject for Federal legislation;

(5) services and goods provided by volunteers and nonprofit organizations would often otherwise be provided by private entities that operate in interstate commerce;

(6) due to high liability costs and unwarranted litigation costs, volunteers and nonprofit organizations face higher costs in purchasing insurance, through interstate insurance markets, to cover their activities; and

(7) clarifying and limiting the liability risk assumed by volunteers is an appropriate subject for Federal legislation because--

(A) of the national scope of the problems created by the legitimate fears of volunteers about frivolous, arbitrary, or capricious lawsuits;

(B) the citizens of the United States depend on, and the Federal Government expends funds on, and provides tax exemptions and other consideration to, numerous social programs that depend on the services of volunteers;

(C) it is in the interest of the Federal Government to encourage the continued operation of volunteer service organizations and contributions of volunteers because the Federal Government lacks the capacity to carry out all of the services provided by such organizations and volunteers; and

(D)(i) liability reform for volunteers, will promote the free flow of goods and services, lessen burdens on interstate commerce and uphold constitutionally protected due process rights; and

(ii) therefore, liability reform is an appropriate use of the powers contained in article 1, section 8, clause 3 of the United States Constitution, and the fourteenth amendment to the United States Constitution.

(b) Purpose

The purpose of this chapter is to promote the interests of social service program beneficiaries and taxpayers and to sustain the availability of programs, nonprofit organizations, and governmental entities that depend on volunteer contributions by reforming the laws to provide certain protections from liability abuses related to volunteers serving nonprofit organizations and governmental entities.

§ 14502. Preemption and election of State nonapplicability

(a) Preemption

This chapter preempts the laws of any State to the extent that such laws are inconsistent with this chapter, except that this chapter shall not preempt any State law that provides additional protection from liability relating to volunteers or to any category of volunteers in the performance of services for a nonprofit organization or governmental entity.

(b) Election of State regarding nonapplicability

This chapter shall not apply to any civil action in a State court against a volunteer in which all parties are citizens of the State if such State enacts a statute in accordance with State requirements for enacting legislation--

(1) citing the authority of this subsection;

(2) declaring the election of such State that this chapter shall not apply, as of a date certain, to such civil action in the State; and

(3) containing no other provisions.

§ 14503. Limitation on liability for volunteers

(a) Liability protection for volunteers

Except as provided in subsections (b) and (d) of this section, no volunteer of a nonprofit organization or governmental entity shall be liable for harm caused by an act or omission of the volunteer on behalf of the organization or entity if--

(1) the volunteer was acting within the scope of the volunteer's responsibilities in the nonprofit organization or governmental entity at the time of the act or omission;

(2) if appropriate or required, the volunteer was properly licensed, certified, or authorized by the appropriate authorities for the activities or practice in the State in which the harm occurred, where the activities were or practice was undertaken within the scope of the volunteer's responsibilities in the nonprofit organization or governmental entity;

(3) the harm was not caused by willful or criminal misconduct, gross negligence, reckless misconduct, or a conscious, flagrant indifference to the rights or safety of the individual harmed by the volunteer; and

(4) the harm was not caused by the volunteer operating a motor vehicle, vessel, aircraft, or other vehicle for which the State requires the operator or the owner of the vehicle, craft, or vessel to--

(A) possess an operator's license; or

(B) maintain insurance.

(b) Concerning responsibility of volunteers to organizations and entities

Nothing in this section shall be construed to affect any civil action brought by any nonprofit organization or any governmental entity against any volunteer of such organization or entity.

(c) No effect on liability of organization or entity

Nothing in this section shall be construed to affect the liability of any nonprofit organization or governmental entity with respect to harm caused to any person.

(d) Exceptions to volunteer liability protection

If the laws of a State limit volunteer liability subject to one or more of the following conditions, such conditions shall not be construed as inconsistent with this section:

(1) A State law that requires a nonprofit organization or governmental entity to adhere to risk management procedures, including mandatory training of volunteers.

(2) A State law that makes the organization or entity liable for the acts or omissions of its volunteers to the same extent as an employer is liable for the acts or omissions of its employees.

(3) A State law that makes a limitation of liability inapplicable if the civil action was brought by an officer of a State or local government pursuant to State or local law.

(4) A State law that makes a limitation of liability applicable only if the nonprofit organization or governmental entity provides a financially secure source of recovery for individuals who suffer harm as a result of actions taken by a volunteer on behalf of the organization or entity. A financially secure source of recovery may be an insurance policy within specified limits, comparable coverage from a risk pooling mechanism, equivalent assets, or alternative arrangements that satisfy the State that the organization or entity will be able to pay for losses up to a specified amount. Separate standards for different types of liability exposure may be specified.

(e) Limitation on punitive damages based on the actions of volunteers

(1) General rule

Punitive damages may not be awarded against a volunteer in an action brought for harm based on the action of a volunteer acting within the scope of the volunteer's responsibilities to a nonprofit organization or governmental entity unless the claimant establishes by clear and convincing evidence that the harm was proximately caused by an action of such volunteer which constitutes willful or criminal misconduct, or a conscious, flagrant indifference to the rights or safety of the individual harmed.

(2) Construction

Paragraph (1) does not create a cause of action for punitive damages and does not preempt or supersede any Federal or State law to the extent that such law would further limit the award of punitive damages.

(f) Exceptions to limitations on liability

(1) In general

The limitations on the liability of a volunteer under this chapter shall not apply to any misconduct that--

(A) constitutes a crime of violence (as that term is defined in section 16 of Title 18) or act of international terrorism (as that term is defined in section 2331 of Title 18) for which the defendant has been convicted in any court;

(B) constitutes a hate crime (as that term is used in the Hate Crime Statistics Act (28 U.S.C. 534 note));

(C) involves a sexual offense, as defined by applicable State law, for which the defendant has been convicted in any court;

(D) involves misconduct for which the defendant has been found to have violated a Federal or State civil rights law; or

(E) where the defendant was under the influence (as determined pursuant to applicable State law) of intoxicating alcohol or any drug at the time of the misconduct.

(2) Rule of construction

Nothing in this subsection shall be construed to effect subsection (a)(3) or (e) of this section.

§ 14504. Liability for noneconomic loss

(a) General rule

In any civil action against a volunteer, based on an action of a volunteer acting within the scope of the volunteer's responsibilities to a nonprofit organization or governmental entity, the liability of the volunteer for noneconomic loss shall be determined in accordance with subsection (b) of this section.

(b) Amount of liability

(1) In general

Each defendant who is a volunteer, shall be liable only for the amount of noneconomic loss allocated to that defendant in direct proportion to the percentage of responsibility of that defendant (determined in accordance with paragraph (2)) for the harm to the claimant with respect to which that defendant is liable. The court shall render a separate judgment against each defendant in an amount determined pursuant to the preceding sentence.

(2) Percentage of responsibility

For purposes of determining the amount of noneconomic loss allocated to a defendant who is a volunteer under this section, the trier of fact shall determine the percentage of responsibility of that defendant for the claimant's harm.

§ 14505. Definitions

For purposes of this chapter:

(1) Economic loss

The term "economic loss" means any pecuniary loss resulting from harm (including the loss of earnings or other benefits related to employment, medical expense loss, replacement services loss, loss due to death, burial costs, and loss of business or employment opportunities) to the extent recovery for such loss is allowed under applicable State law.

(2) Harm

The term "harm" includes physical, nonphysical, economic, and noneconomic losses.

(3) Noneconomic losses

The term "noneconomic losses" means losses for physical and emotional pain, suffering, inconvenience, physical impairment, mental anguish, disfigurement, loss of enjoyment of life, loss of society and companionship, loss of consortium (other than loss of domestic service), hedonic damages, injury to reputation and all other nonpecuniary losses of any kind or nature.

(4) Nonprofit organization

The term "nonprofit organization" means--

(A) any organization which is described in section 501(c)(3) of Title 26 and exempt from tax under section 501(a) of Title 26 and which does not practice any action which constitutes a hate crime referred to in subsection (b)(1) of the first section of the Hate Crime Statistics Act (28 U.S.C. 534 note); or

(B) any not-for-profit organization which is organized and conducted for public benefit and operated primarily for charitable, civic, educational, religious, welfare, or health purposes and which does not practice any action which constitutes a hate crime referred to in subsection (b)(1) of the first section of the Hate Crime Statistics Act (28 U.S.C. 534 note).

(5) State

The term "State" means each of the several States, the District of Columbia, the Commonwealth of Puerto Rico, the Virgin Islands, Guam, American Samoa, the Northern Mariana Islands, any other territory or possession of the United States, or any political subdivision of any such State, territory, or possession.

(6) Volunteer

The term "volunteer" means an individual performing services for a nonprofit organization or a governmental entity who does not receive--

(A) compensation (other than reasonable reimbursement or allowance for expenses actually incurred); or

(B) any other thing of value in lieu of compensation, in excess of $500 per year, and such term includes a volunteer serving as a director, officer, trustee, or direct service volunteer.

TREASURY REGULATIONS ON INCOME TAX

Prop. Reg. § 1.512(a)-1. Definition.

* * *

Example 2. (i) P, a manufacturer of photographic equipment, underwrites a photography exhibition organized by M, an art museum described in section 501(c)(3). In return for a payment of $100,000, M agrees that the exhibition catalog sold by M in connection with the exhibit will advertise P's product. The exhibition catalog will also include educational material, such as copies of photographs included in the exhibition, interviews with photographers, and an essay by the curator of M's department of photography. For purposes of this example, assume that none of the $100,000 is a qualified sponsorship payment within the meaning of section 513(i) and section 1.513-4, that M's advertising activity is regularly carried on, and that the entire amount of the payment is unrelated business taxable income to M. Expenses directly connected with generating the unrelated business taxable income (i.e., direct advertising costs) total $25,000. Expenses directly connected with the preparation and publication of the exhibition catalog (other than direct advertising costs) total $110,000. M receives $60,000 of gross revenue from sales of the exhibition catalog. Expenses directly connected with the conduct of the exhibition total $500,000.

(ii) The computation of unrelated business taxable income is as follows:

(A) Unrelated trade or business (sale of advertising):

Income	$ 100,000
Directly-connected expenses	(25,000)
Subtotal	$ 75,000

(B) Exempt function (publication of exhibition catalog):

Income (from catalog sales)	$ 60,000
Directly-connected expenses	(110,000)
Net exempt function income (loss)	($50,000)
Unrelated business taxable income	$ 25,000

(iii) **Expenses related to publication of the exhibition catalog exceed revenues by $50,000.**   Because the unrelated business activity (the sale of advertising) exploits an exempt activity (the publication of the exhibition catalog),

69

and because the publication of editorial material is an activity normally conducted by taxable entities that sell advertising, the net loss from the exempt publication activity is allowed as a deduction from unrelated business income under paragraph (d)(2) of this section. In contrast, the presentation of an exhibition is not an activity normally conducted by taxable entities engaged in advertising and publication activity for purposes of paragraph (d)(2) of this section. Consequently, the $500,000 cost of presenting the exhibition is not directly connected with the conduct of the unrelated advertising activity and does not have a proximate and primary relationship to that activity. Accordingly, M has unrelated business taxable income of $25,000.

Prop. Reg. § 1.513-4. Certain Sponsorship Not Unrelated Trade or Business.

(a) In general. Under section 513(i), the receipt of qualified sponsorship payments by an exempt organization which is subject to the tax imposed by section 511 does not constitute receipt of income from an unrelated trade or business.

(b) Exception. The provisions of this section do not apply with respect to payments made in connection with qualified convention and trade show activities. For rules governing qualified convention and trade show activity, see section 1.513-3. The provisions of this section also do not apply to income derived from the sale of advertising or acknowledgments in exempt organization periodicals. For this purpose, the term periodical means regularly scheduled and printed material published by or on behalf of the exempt organization that is not related to and primarily distributed in connection with a specific event conducted by the exempt organization. For rules governing the sale of advertising in exempt organization periodicals, see section 1.512(a)-1(f).

(c) Qualified sponsorship payment--(1) Definition. The term qualified sponsorship payment means any payment of money, transfer of property, or performance of services by any person engaged in a trade or business with respect to which there is no arrangement or expectation that the person will receive any substantial return benefit. In determining whether a payment is a qualified sponsorship payment, it is irrelevant whether the sponsored activity is related or unrelated to the recipient organization's exempt purpose. It is also irrelevant whether the sponsored activity is temporary or permanent.

(2) Substantial return benefit--(i) In general. For purposes of this section, a substantial return benefit means any benefit other than goods, services or other benefits of insubstantial value that are disregarded under paragraph (c)(2)(ii) of this section, or a use or acknowledgment described in paragraph (c)(2)(iii) of this section. A substantial return benefit includes advertising as defined in paragraph (c)(2)(iv) of this section, providing facilities, services or other privileges to the payor or persons designated by the payor (except as provided in paragraph (c)(2)(ii) of this section), and granting the payor or persons designated by the payor an exclusive or nonexclusive right to use an intangible asset (e.g., trademark, patent, logo, or designation) of the exempt organization.

(ii) Certain goods or services disregarded. (A) For purposes of paragraph (c)(2)(i) of this section, goods, services or other benefits are disregarded if:

(1) The goods, services or other benefits provided to the payor or persons designated by the payor have an aggregate fair market value of not more than 2% of the amount of the payment, or $74 (adjusted for tax years beginning after calendar year 2000 by an amount determined under section 1(f)(3), by substituting "calendar year 1999" for "calendar year 1992" in section 1(f)(3)(B)), whichever is less (or such other amount(s) as may be specified in a revenue procedure or other form of guidance issued by the Commissioner); or

(2) The only benefits provided to the payor or persons designated by the payor are token items (e.g., bookmarks, calendars, key chains, mugs, posters, tee shirts) bearing the exempt organization's name or logo that have an aggregate cost within the limit established for low cost articles under section 513(h)(2) (or such other limit as may be specified in a revenue procedure or other form of guidance issued by the Commissioner); however, token items (as described above) provided to employees of the payor, or to partners of a partnership that is the payor, are disregarded if the combined total cost of the token items provided to each employee or partner does not exceed the limit stated in this paragraph (c)(2)(ii)(A)(2).

(B) If the fair market value of the benefits (or the cost, in the case of token items) exceeds the amount or limit specified in paragraph (c)(2)(ii)(A) of this section, then (except as provided in paragraph (c)(2)(iii) of this section) the entire fair market value (as opposed to cost) of such benefits, not merely the excess amount, is a substantial return benefit.

(iii) Use or acknowledgment. For purposes of this section, a substantial return benefit does not include the use or acknowledgment of the name or logo (or product lines) of the payor's trade or business in connection with the activities of the exempt organization. Use or acknowledgment does not include advertising as described in paragraph (c)(2)(iv) of this section, but may include the following: logos and slogans that do not contain qualitative or comparative descriptions of the payor's products, services, facilities or company; a list of the payor's locations, telephone numbers, or Internet address; value-neutral descriptions, including displays or visual depictions, of the payor's product-line or services; and the payor's brand or trade names and product or service listings. Logos or slogans that are an established part of a payor's identity are not considered to contain qualitative or comparative descriptions. Mere display or distribution, whether for free or remuneration, of a payor's product by the payor or the exempt organization to the general public at the sponsored activity is not considered an inducement to purchase, sell or use the payor's product for purposes of this section and, thus, will not affect the determination of whether a payment is a qualified sponsorship payment.

(iv) **Advertising.** For purposes of this section, the term advertising means any message or other programming material which is broadcast or otherwise transmitted, published, displayed or distributed, and which promotes or markets any trade or business, or any service, facility or product. Advertising includes messages containing qualitative or comparative language, price information or other indications of savings or value, an endorsement, or an inducement to purchase, sell, or use any company, service, facility or product. A single message that contains both advertising and an acknowledgment is advertising. This section does not apply to activities conducted by a payor on its own. For example, if a payor purchases broadcast time from a television station to advertise its product during commercial breaks in a sponsored program, the exempt organization's activities are not thereby converted to advertising.

(v) **Exclusivity arrangements -- (A) Exclusive sponsor**. An arrangement that acknowledges the payor as the exclusive sponsor of an exempt organization's activity, or the exclusive sponsor representing a particular trade, business or industry, generally does not, by itself, result in a substantial return benefit. For example, if in exchange for a payment, an organization announces that its event is sponsored exclusively by the payor (and does not provide any advertising or other substantial return benefit to the payor), the payor has not received a substantial return benefit.

(B) **Exclusive provider**. An arrangement that limits the sale, distribution, availability, or use of competing products, services, or facilities in connection with an exempt organization's activity generally results in a substantial return benefit. For example, if in exchange for a payment, the exempt organization agrees to allow only the payor's products to be sold in connection with an activity, the payor has received a substantial return benefit.

(d) **Allocation of payment -- (1) In general**. If there is an arrangement or expectation that the payor will receive a substantial return benefit with respect to any payment, then only the portion, if any, of the payment that exceeds the fair market value of the substantial return benefit (determined on the date the sponsorship arrangement is entered into) is a qualified sponsorship payment. However, if the exempt organization does not establish that the payment exceeds the fair market value of any substantial return benefit, then no portion of the payment constitutes a qualified sponsorship payment. The unrelated business income tax (UBIT) treatment of any payment (or portion thereof) that is not a qualified sponsorship payment is determined by application of sections 512, 513 and 514. For example, payments related to an exempt organization's providing facilities, services, or other privileges to the payor or persons designated by the payor, advertising, exclusive provider arrangements described in paragraph (c)(2)(v)(B) of this section, a license to use intangible assets of the exempt organization, or other substantial return benefits, are evaluated separately in determining whether the exempt organization realizes unrelated business taxable income. The fair market value of any substantial return benefit provided as part of a sponsorship arrangement is the price at which the benefit would be provided between a willing recipient and a willing provider of the benefit, neither being under any compulsion to enter into the arrangement, and both having reasonable knowledge of relevant facts, and without regard to any other aspect of the sponsorship arrangement.

(2) Anti-abuse provision. To the extent necessary to prevent avoidance of the rule stated in paragraph (d)(1) of this section, where the exempt organization fails to make a reasonable and good faith valuation of any substantial return benefit, the Commissioner (or the Commissioner's delegate) may determine the portion of a payment allocable to such substantial return benefit and may treat two or more related payments as a single payment.

(e) Special rules--(1) Written agreements. The existence of a written sponsorship agreement does not, in itself, cause a payment to fail to be a qualified sponsorship payment. The terms of the agreement, not its existence or degree of detail, are relevant to the determination of whether a payment is a qualified sponsorship payment. Similarly, the terms of the agreement and not the title or responsibilities of the individuals negotiating the agreement determine whether a payment (or any portion thereof) made pursuant to the agreement is a qualified sponsorship payment.

(2) Contingent payments. The term qualified sponsorship payment does not include any payment the amount of which is contingent, by contract or otherwise, upon the level of attendance at one or more events, broadcast ratings, or other factors indicating the degree of public exposure to the sponsored activity. The fact that a payment is contingent upon sponsored events or activities actually being conducted does not, by itself, cause the payment to fail to be a qualified sponsorship payment.

(3) Determining public support. Qualified sponsorship payments in the form of money or property (but not services) are treated as contributions received by the exempt organization for purposes of determining public support to the organization under section 170(b)(1)(A)(vi) or section 509(a)(2). See sections 1.509(a)-3(f)(1) and 1.170A-9(e)(6)(i). The fact that a payment is a qualified sponsorship payment that is treated as a contribution to the payee organization does not determine whether the payment is deductible by the payor under section 162 or section 170.

(f) Examples. The provisions of this section are illustrated by the following examples. The tax treatment of any payment (or portion of a payment) that does not constitute a qualified sponsorship payment is governed by general UBIT principles. In these examples, the recipients of the payments at issue are section 501(c) organizations. The only benefits received by the payors are those specifically indicated in the example. The examples are as follows:

Example 1. M, a local charity, organizes a marathon and walkathon at which it serves to participants drinks and other refreshments provided free of charge by a national corporation. The corporation also gives M prizes to be awarded to winners of the event. M recognizes the assistance of the corporation by listing the corporation's name in promotional fliers, in newspaper advertisements of the event and on T-shirts worn by participants. M changes the name of its event to include the name of the corporation. M's activities constitute acknowledgment of the sponsorship. The drinks, refreshments and prizes provided by the corporation are a qualified sponsorship payment, which is not income from an unrelated trade or business.

Example 2. N, an art museum, organizes an exhibition and receives a large payment from a corporation to help fund the exhibition. N recognizes the corporation's support by using the corporate name and established logo in materials publicizing the exhibition, including banners, posters, brochures and public service announcements. N also hosts a dinner for the corporation's executives. The fair market value of the dinner exceeds the amount specified in paragraph (c)(2)(ii) of this section. N's use of the corporate name and logo in connection with the exhibition constitutes acknowledgment of the sponsorship. However, the dinner for corporate executives is a substantial return benefit. Only that portion of the payment, if any, that N can demonstrate exceeds the fair market value of the dinner is a qualified sponsorship payment.

Example 3. O coordinates sports tournaments for local charities. An auto manufacturer agrees to underwrite the expenses of the tournaments. O recognizes the auto manufacturer by including the manufacturer's name and established logo in the title of each tournament as well as on signs, scoreboards and other printed material. The auto manufacturer receives complimentary admission passes and pro-am playing spots for each tournament that have a fair market value in excess of the amount specified in paragraph (c)(2)(ii) of this section. Additionally, O displays the latest models of the manufacturer's premier luxury cars at each tournament. O's use of the manufacturer's name and logo and display of cars in the tournament area constitute acknowledgment of the sponsorship. However, the admission passes and pro-am playing spots are a substantial return benefit. Only that portion of the payment, if any, that O can demonstrate exceeds the fair market value of the admission passes and pro-am playing spots is a qualified sponsorship payment.

Example 4. P conducts an annual college football bowl game. P sells to commercial broadcasters the right to broadcast the bowl game on television and radio. A major corporation agrees to be the exclusive sponsor of the bowl game. The detailed contract between P and the corporation provides that the name of the bowl game will include the name of the corporation. The contract further provides that the corporation's name and established logo will appear on players' helmets and uniforms, on the scoreboard and stadium signs, on the playing field, on cups used to serve drinks at the game, and on all related printed material distributed in connection with the game. The agreement is contingent upon the game being broadcast on television and radio, but the amount of the payment is not contingent upon the number of people attending the game or the television ratings. The contract provides that television cameras will focus on the corporation's name and logo on the field at certain intervals during the game. P's use of the corporation's name and logo in connection with the bowl game constitutes acknowledgment of the sponsorship. The exclusive sponsorship arrangement is not a substantial return benefit. The entire payment is a qualified sponsorship payment, which is not income from an unrelated trade or business.

Example 5. Q organizes an amateur sports team. A major pizza chain gives uniforms to players on Q's team, and also pays some of the team's operational expenses. The uniforms bear the name and established logo of the pizza chain. During the final tournament series, Q distributes free of charge souvenir flags bearing Q's name to employees of the pizza chain who come out to support the team. The flags cost $2 each. The flags are not a substantial return benefit because they are token items that qualify as low cost articles under paragraph (c)(2)(ii) of this section. Q's use of the name and logo of the pizza chain in connection with the tournament constitutes acknowledgment of the sponsorship. The funding and supplied uniforms are a qualified sponsorship payment, which is not income from an unrelated trade or business.

Example 6. R is a liberal arts college. A soft drink manufacturer makes a substantial payment to the college's English department, and in exchange, R names a writing competition after the soft drink manufacturer. In addition, R agrees to limit all soft drink sales on campus to the manufacturer's brand of soft drink. R's use of the manufacturer's name in the writing competition constitutes acknowledgment of the sponsorship. However, limiting all soft drink sales on campus to the manufacturer's brand of soft drink, i.e., the exclusive provider arrangement, is a substantial return benefit. Only that portion of the payment, if any, that R can demonstrate exceeds the fair market value of the exclusive provider arrangement is a qualified sponsorship payment.

Example 7. S is a noncommercial broadcast station that airs a program funded by a local music store. In exchange for the funding, S broadcasts the following message: "This program has been brought to you by the Music Shop, located at 123 Main Street. For your music needs, give them a call today at 555-1234. This station is proud to have the Music Shop as a sponsor." Because this single broadcast message contains both advertising and an acknowledgment, the entire message is advertising and constitutes a substantial return benefit. Unless S establishes that the amount of the payment exceeds the fair market value of the advertising, none of the payment is a qualified sponsorship payment.

Example 8. T, a symphony orchestra, performs a series of concerts. A program guide that contains notes on guest conductors and other information concerning the evening's program is distributed by T at each concert. The Music Shop makes a payment to T in support of the concert series. As a supporter of the event, the Music Shop is recognized in the program guide and on a poster in the lobby of the concert hall. The Music Shop receives complimentary tickets to the concert series. The fair market value of the complimentary tickets exceeds the amount specified in paragraph (c)(2)(ii) of this section. The lobby poster states that "The T concert is sponsored by the Music Shop, located at 123 Main Street, telephone number 555-1234." The program guide contains the same information and also states, "Visit today for the finest selection of music CDs and cassette tapes." T's use of the Music Shop's name and address in the lobby poster constitutes acknowledgment of the sponsorship. However, the promotion in the program guide and complimentary tickets are a substantial return benefit. Only that portion of the payment, if any, that T can demonstrate exceeds the fair market value of the promotion in the program guide and complimentary tickets is a qualified sponsorship payment.

Example 9. U, a national charity dedicated to promoting health, organizes a campaign to inform the public about potential cures to fight a serious disease. As part of the campaign, U sends representatives to community health fairs around the country to answer questions about the disease and inform the public about recent developments in the search for a cure. A pharmaceutical company makes a payment to U to fund U's booth at a health fair. U places a sign in the booth displaying the pharmaceutical company's name and slogan, "Better Research, Better Health," which is an established part of the company's identity. In addition, U grants the pharmaceutical company a license to use U's logo in marketing its products to health care providers around the country. U's display of the pharmaceutical company's name and slogan constitutes acknowledgment of the sponsorship. However, the license granted to the pharmaceutical company to use U's logo is a substantial return benefit. Only that portion of the payment, if any, that U can demonstrate exceeds the fair market value of the license granted to the pharmaceutical company is a qualified sponsorship payment.

Example 10. V, a trade association, publishes a monthly scientific magazine for its members containing information about current issues and developments in the field. A textbook publisher makes a large payment to V to have its name displayed on the inside cover of the magazine each month. Because the monthly magazine is a periodical within the meaning of paragraph (b) of this section, the section 513(i) safe harbor does not apply. See section 1.512(a)-1(f).

Prop. Reg. § 1.513-7.   Travel and Tour Activities of Tax Exempt Organizations.

(a) Travel tour activities that constitute a trade or business, as defined in section 1.513(b), and that are not substantially related to the purposes for which exemption has been granted to the organization constitute an unrelated trade or business with respect to that organization. Whether travel tour activities conducted by an organization are substantially related to the organization's exempt purpose is determined by looking at all relevant facts and circumstances. Section 513(c) and section 1.513-1(b) also apply to travel tour activity. Application of the rules of section 513(c) and section 1.513-1(b) may result in different treatment for individual tours within an organization's travel tour program.

(b) **Examples.** The provisions of this section are illustrated by the following examples:

Example 1. O, a university alumni association, is exempt from federal income tax under section 501(a) as an educational organization described in section 501(c)(3). As part of its activities, O operates a travel tour program. The program is open to all current members of O and their guests. O works with travel agencies to schedule approximately 10 tours annually to various destinations around the world. Members of O pay $X to the organizing travel agency to participate in a tour. The travel agency pays O a per person fee for each participant. Although the literature advertising the tours encourages O's members to continue their lifelong learning by joining the tours, and a faculty member of O's related university is invited to join the tour as a guest of the alumni association, none of the tours includes any scheduled instruction or curriculum related to the destinations being visited. By arranging to make travel tours available to its members, O is not contributing importantly to the accomplishment of its educational purpose. Rather, O's program is designed to generate revenues for O by regularly offering its members travel services. Accordingly, O's tour program is an unrelated trade or business within the meaning of section 513(a) of the Code.

Example 2. N is an organization formed for the purpose of educating individuals about the geography and culture of the United States. It is exempt from federal income tax under section 501(a) as an educational and cultural organization described in section 501(c)(3). N engages in a number of activities to accomplish its purposes, including offering courses and publishing periodicals and books. As one of its activities, N conducts study tours to national parks and other locations within the United States. The study tours are conducted by teachers and other education professionals. The tours are open to all who agree to participate in the required study program. The study program consists of community college level courses related to the location being visited by the tour. While the students are on the tour, five or six hours per day are devoted to organized study, preparation of reports, lectures, instruction and recitation by the students. Each tour group brings along a library of material related to the subject being studied on the tour. Examinations are given at the end of each tour and N's state board of education awards academic credit for tour participation. Because the tours offered by N include a substantial amount of required study, lectures, report preparation, examinations and qualify for academic credit, the tours clearly further N's educational purpose. Accordingly, N's tour program is not an unrelated trade or business within the meaning of section 513(a) of the Code.

Example 3. R is a section 501(c)(4) social welfare organization devoted to advocacy on a particular issue. On a regular basis throughout the year, R organizes a travel tour for its members to Washington, D.C. The tours are priced to produce a profit for R. While in Washington, the members follow a schedule according to which they spend substantially all of their time over several days attending meetings with legislators and government officials and receiving briefings on policy developments related to the issue that is R's focus. Bringing members to Washington to participate in advocacy on behalf of the organization and learn about developments relating to the organization's principal focus is substantially related to R's social welfare purpose. Therefore, R's operation of the travel tours does not constitute an unrelated trade or business.

Example 4. S is a membership organization formed to foster cultural unity and to educate X Americans about X, their country of origin. It is exempt from federal income tax under section 501(a) and is described in section 501(c)(3) as an educational and cultural organization. Membership in S is open to all Americans interested in the X heritage. As part of its activities, S sponsors a program of travel tours to X. All of S's tours are priced to produce a profit for S. The tours are divided into two categories. Category A tours are trips to X that are designed to immerse participants in the X history, culture and language. The itinerary is designed to have participants spend substantially all of their time while in X receiving instruction on the X language, history and cultural heritage. Destinations are selected because of their historical or cultural significance or because of instructional resources they offer. Category B tours are also trips to X, but rather than offering scheduled instruction, participants are given the option of taking guided tours of various X locations included in their itinerary. Other than the optional guided tours, Category B tours offer no instruction or curriculum. Even if participants take all of the tours offered, they have a substantial amount of time free to pursue their own interests once in X. Destinations of principally recreational interest, rather than historical or cultural interest, are regularly included on Category B tour itineraries. Based on the facts and circumstances, sponsoring Category A tours is an activity substantially related to S's exempt purposes, and does not constitute an unrelated trade or business with respect to S. However, sponsoring Category B tours does not contribute importantly to S's accomplishment of its exempt purposes and is designed to generate a profit for S. Therefore, sponsoring the Category B tours constitutes an unrelated trade or business with respect to S.

* * *

Temp. Reg. § 53.4958-1T. Taxes on excess benefit transactions

(a) **In general**. Section 4958 imposes excise taxes on each excess benefit transaction (as defined in section 4958(c) and section 53.4958-4T) between an applicable tax-exempt organization (as defined in section 4958(e) and section 53.4958-2T) and a disqualified person (as defined in section 4958(f)(1) and section 53.4958-3T). A disqualified person who receives an excess benefit from an excess benefit transaction is liable for payment of a section 4958(a)(1) excise tax equal to 25 percent of the excess benefit. If an initial tax is imposed by section 4958(a)(1) on an excess benefit transaction and the transaction is not corrected (as defined in section 4958(f)(6) and section 53.4958-7T) within the taxable period (as defined in section 4958(f)(5) and paragraph (c)(2)(ii) of this section), then any disqualified person who received an excess benefit from the excess benefit transaction on which the initial tax was imposed is liable for an additional tax of 200 percent of the excess benefit. An organization manager (as defined in section 4958(f)(2) and paragraph (d) of this section) who participates in an excess benefit transaction, knowing that it was such a transaction, is liable for payment of a section 4958(a)(2) excise tax equal to 10 percent of the excess benefit, unless the participation was not willful and was due to reasonable cause. If an organization manager also receives an excess benefit from an excess benefit transaction, the manager may be liable for both taxes imposed by section 4958(a).

(b) **Excess benefit defined**. An excess benefit is the amount by which the value of the economic benefit provided by an applicable tax-exempt organization directly or indirectly to or for the use of any disqualified person exceeds the value of the consideration (including the performance of services) received for providing such benefit.

(c) Taxes paid by disqualified person--(1) Initial tax. Section 4958(a)(1) imposes a tax equal to 25 percent of the excess benefit on each excess benefit transaction. The section 4958(a)(1) tax shall be paid by any disqualified person who received an excess benefit from that excess benefit transaction. With respect to any excess benefit transaction, if more than one disqualified person is liable for the tax imposed by section 4958(a)(1), all such persons are jointly and severally liable for that tax.

(2) Additional tax on disqualified person--(i) In general. Section 4958(b) imposes a tax equal to 200 percent of the excess benefit in any case in which section 4958(a)(1) imposes a 25-percent tax on an excess benefit transaction and the transaction is not corrected (as defined in section 4958(f)(6) and section 53.4958-7T) within the taxable period (as defined in section 4958(f)(5) and paragraph (c)(2)(ii) of this section). If a disqualified person makes a payment of less than the full correction amount under the rules of section 53.4958-7T, the 200-percent tax is imposed only on the unpaid portion of the correction amount (as described in section 53.4958- 7T(c)). The tax imposed by section 4958(b) is payable by any disqualified person who received an excess benefit from the excess benefit transaction on which the initial tax was imposed by section 4958(a)(1). With respect to any excess benefit transaction, if more than one disqualified person is liable for the tax imposed by section 4958(b), all such persons are jointly and severally liable for that tax.

(ii) Taxable period. Taxable period means, with respect to any excess benefit transaction, the period beginning with the date on which the transaction occurs and ending on the earlier of --

(A) The date of mailing a notice of deficiency under section 6212 with respect to the section 4958(a)(1) tax; or

(B) The date on which the tax imposed by section 4958(a)(1) is assessed.

(iii) Abatement if correction during the correction period. For rules relating to abatement of taxes on excess benefit transactions that are corrected within the correction period, as defined in section 4963(e), see sections 4961(a), 4962(a), and the regulations thereunder. The abatement rules of section 4961 specifically provide for a 90-day correction period after the date of mailing a notice of deficiency under section 6212 with respect to the section 4958(b) 200-percent tax. If the excess benefit is corrected during that correction period, the 200-percent tax imposed shall not be assessed, and if assessed the assessment shall be abated, and if collected shall be credited or refunded as an overpayment. For special rules relating to abatement of the 25-percent tax, see section 4962.

(d) Tax paid by organization managers--(1) In general. In any case in which section 4958(a)(1) imposes a tax, section 4958(a)(2) imposes a tax equal to 10 percent of the excess benefit on the participation of any organization manager who knowingly participated in the excess benefit transaction, unless such participation was not willful and was due to reasonable cause. Any organization manager who so participated in the excess benefit transaction must pay the tax.

(2) Organization manager defined--(i) In general. An organization manager is, with respect to any applicable tax-exempt organization, any officer, director, or trustee of such organization, or any individual having powers or responsibilities similar to those of officers, directors, or trustees of the organization, regardless of title. A person is an officer of an organization if that person --

(A) Is specifically so designated under the certificate of incorporation, by-laws, or other constitutive documents of the organization; or

(B) Regularly exercises general authority to make administrative or policy decisions on behalf of the organization. An independent contractor who acts solely in a capacity as an attorney, accountant, or investment manager or advisor, is not an officer. For purposes of this paragraph (d)(2)(i)(B), any person who has authority merely to recommend particular administrative or policy decisions, but not to implement them without approval of a superior, is not an officer.

(ii) Special rule for certain committee members. An individual who is not an officer, director, or trustee, yet serves on a committee of the governing body of an applicable tax-exempt organization (or as a designee of the governing body described in section 53.4958-6T(c)(1)) that is attempting to invoke the rebuttable presumption of reasonableness described in section 53.4958-6T based on the committee's (or designee's) actions, is an organization manager for purposes of the tax imposed by section 4958(a)(2).

(3) Participation. For purposes of section 4958(a)(2) and paragraph (d) of this section, participation includes silence or inaction on the part of an organization manager where the manager is under a duty to speak or act, as well as any affirmative action by such manager. An organization manager is not considered to have participated in an excess benefit transaction, however, where the manager has opposed the transaction in a manner consistent with the fulfillment of the manager's responsibilities to the applicable tax-exempt organization.

(4) Knowing--(i) In general. For purposes of section 4958(a)(2) and paragraph (d) of this section, a manager participates in a transaction knowingly only if the person--

(A) Has actual knowledge of sufficient facts so that, based solely upon those facts, such transaction would be an excess benefit transaction;

(B) Is aware that such a transaction under these circumstances may violate the provisions of federal tax law governing excess benefit transactions; and

(C) Negligently fails to make reasonable attempts to ascertain whether the transaction is an excess benefit transaction, or the manager is in fact aware that it is such a transaction.

(ii) Amplification of general rule. Knowing does not mean having reason to know. However, evidence tending to show that a manager has reason to know of a particular fact or particular rule is relevant in determining whether the manager had actual knowledge of such a fact or rule. Thus, for example, evidence tending to show that a manager has reason to know of sufficient facts so that, based solely upon such facts, a transaction would be an excess benefit transaction is relevant in determining whether the manager has actual knowledge of such facts.

(iii) Reliance on professional advice. An organization manager's participation in a transaction is ordinarily not considered knowing within the meaning of section 4958(a)(2), even though the transaction is subsequently held to be an excess benefit transaction to the extent that, after full disclosure of the factual situation to an appropriate professional, the organization manager relies on a reasoned written opinion of that professional with respect to elements of the transaction within the professional's expertise. For purposes of section 4958(a)(2) and this paragraph (d), a written opinion is reasoned even though it reaches a conclusion that is subsequently determined to be incorrect so long as the opinion addresses itself to the facts and the applicable standards. However, a written opinion is not reasoned if it does nothing more than recite the facts and express a conclusion. The absence of a written opinion of an appropriate professional with respect to a transaction shall not, by itself, however, give rise to any inference that an organization manager participated in the transaction knowingly. For purposes of this paragraph, appropriate professionals on whose written opinion an organization manager may rely, are limited to --

(A) Legal counsel, including in-house counsel;

(B) Certified public accountants or accounting firms with expertise regarding the relevant tax law matters; and

(C) Independent valuation experts who--

(1) Hold themselves out to the public as appraisers or compensation consultants;

(2) Perform the relevant valuations on a regular basis;

(3) Are qualified to make valuations of the type of property or services involved; and

(4) Include in the written opinion a certification that the requirements of paragraphs (d)(4)(iii)(C)(1) through (3) of this section are met.

(iv) Reliance on rebuttable presumption of reasonableness. An organization manager's participation in a transaction is ordinarily not considered knowing within the meaning of section 4958(a)(2), even though the transaction is subsequently held to be an excess benefit transaction, if the organization manager relies on the fact that the requirements of section 53.4958-6T(a) are satisfied with respect to the transaction.

(5) Willful. For purposes of section 4958(a)(2) and this paragraph (d), participation by an organization manager is willful if it is voluntary, conscious, and intentional. No motive to avoid the restrictions of the law or the incurrence of any tax is necessary to make the participation willful. However, participation by an organization manager is not willful if the manager does not know that the transaction in which the manager is participating is an excess benefit transaction.

(6) Due to reasonable cause. An organization manager's participation is due to reasonable cause if the manager has exercised responsibility on behalf of the organization with ordinary business care and prudence.

(7) Limits on liability for management. The maximum aggregate amount of tax collectible under section 4958(a)(2) and this paragraph (d) from organization managers with respect to any one excess benefit transaction is $10,000.

(8) Joint and several liability. In any case where more than one person is liable for a tax imposed by section 4958(a)(2), all such persons shall be jointly and severally liable for the taxes imposed under section 4958(a)(2) with respect to that excess benefit transaction.

(9) Burden of proof. For provisions relating to the burden of proof in cases involving the issue of whether an organization manager has knowingly participated in an excess benefit transaction, see section 7454(b) and section 301.7454-2. In these cases, the Commissioner bears the burden of proof.

(e) Date of occurrence--(1) In general. Except as otherwise provided, an excess benefit transaction occurs on the date on which the disqualified person receives the economic benefit for Federal income tax purposes. When a single contractual arrangement provides for a series of compensation or other payments to (or for the use of) a disqualified person over the course of the disqualified person's taxable year (or part of a taxable year), any excess benefit transaction with respect to these aggregate payments is deemed to occur on the last day of the taxable year (or if the payments continue for part of the year, the date of the last payment in the series).

(2) Special rules. In the case of benefits provided pursuant to a qualified pension, profit-sharing, or stock bonus plan, the transaction occurs on the date the benefit is vested. In the case of a transfer of property that is subject to a substantial risk of forfeiture or in the case of rights to future compensation or property (including benefits under a nonqualified deferred compensation plan), the transaction occurs on the date the property, or the rights to future compensation or property, is not subject to a substantial risk of forfeiture. However, where the disqualified person elects to include an amount in gross income in the taxable year of transfer pursuant to section 83(b), the general rule of paragraph (e)(1) of this section applies to the property with respect to which the section 83(b) election is made. Any excess benefit transaction with respect to benefits under a deferred compensation plan which vest during any taxable year of the disqualified person is deemed to occur on the last day of such taxable year. For the rules governing the timing of the reasonableness determination for deferred, contingent, and certain other noncash compensation, see section 53.4958-4T(b)(2).

(3) Statute of limitations rules. See sections 6501(e)(3) and 6501(l) and the regulations thereunder for statute of limitations rules as they apply to section 4958 excise taxes.

(f) Effective date for imposition of taxes--(1) In general. The section 4958 taxes imposed on excess benefit transactions or on participation in excess benefit transactions apply to transactions occurring on or after September 14, 1995.

* * *

Temp. Reg. § 53.4958-2T. Definition of applicable tax-exempt organization

(a) Organizations described in section 501(c)(3) or (4) and exempt from tax under section 501(a)--(1) In general. An applicable tax-exempt organization is any organization that, without regard to any excess benefit, would be described in section 501(c)(3) or (4) and exempt from tax under section 501(a). An applicable tax-exempt organization also includes any organization that was described in section 501(c)(3) or (4) and was exempt from tax under section 501(a) at any time during a five-year period ending on the date of an excess benefit transaction (the lookback period). A private foundation as defined in section 509(a) is not an applicable tax-exempt organization for section 4958 purposes. A governmental entity that is exempt from (or not subject to) taxation without regard to section 501(a) is not an applicable tax-exempt organization for section 4958 purposes.

(2) Organizations described in section 501(c)(3). An organization is described in section 501(c)(3) for purposes of section 4958 only if the organization provides the notice described in section 508, unless the organization otherwise is described in section 501(c)(3) and specifically is excluded from the requirements of section 508 by that section.

(3) Organizations described in section 501(c)(4). An organization is described in section 501(c)(4) for purposes of section 4958 if the organization--

(i) Has applied for and received recognition from the Internal Revenue Service as an organization described in section 501(c)(4); or

(ii) Has filed an application for recognition under section 501(c)(4) with the Internal Revenue Service, has filed an annual information return as a section 501(c)(4) organization under the Internal Revenue Code or regulations promulgated thereunder, or has otherwise held itself out as being described in section 501(c)(4) and exempt from tax under section 501(a).

(4) Effect of non-recognition or revocation of exempt status. An organization is not described in paragraph (a)(2) or (3) of this section during any period covered by a final determination or adjudication that the organization is not exempt from tax under section 501(a) as an organization described in section 501(c)(3) or (4), so long as that determination or adjudication is not based upon participation in inurement or one or more excess benefit transactions. However, the organization may be an applicable tax- exempt organization for that period as a result of the five-year lookback rule described in paragraph (a)(1) of this section.

(b) Special rules--(1) Transition rule for lookback period. In the case of any excess benefit transaction occurring before September 14, 2000, the lookback period described in paragraph (a)(1) of this section begins on September 14, 1995, and ends on the date of the transaction.

(2) Certain foreign organizations. A foreign organization, recognized by the Internal Revenue Service or by treaty, that receives substantially all of its support (other than gross investment income) from sources outside of the United States is not an organization described in section 501(c)(3) or (4) for purposes of section 4958.

Temp. Reg. § 53.4958-3T. Definition of disqualified person

(a) In general--(1) Scope of definition. Section 4958(f)(1) defines disqualified person, with respect to any transaction, as any person who was in a position to exercise substantial influence over the affairs of an applicable tax-exempt organization at any time during the five-year period ending on the date of the transaction (the lookback period). Paragraph (b) of this section describes persons who are defined to be disqualified persons under the statute, including certain family members of an individual in a position to exercise substantial influence, and certain 35-percent controlled entities. Paragraph (c) of this section describes persons in a position to exercise substantial influence over the affairs of an applicable tax-exempt organization by virtue of their powers and responsibilities or certain interests they hold. Paragraph (d) of this section describes persons deemed not to be in a position to exercise substantial influence. Whether any person who is not described in paragraph (b), (c) or (d) of this section is a disqualified person with respect to a transaction for purposes of section 4958 is based on all relevant facts and circumstances, as described in paragraph (e) of this section. Paragraph (f) of this section describes special rules for affiliated organizations. Examples in paragraph (g) of this section illustrate these categories of persons.

(2) Transition rule for lookback period. In the case of any excess benefit transaction occurring before September 14, 2000, the lookback period described in paragraph (a)(1) of this section begins on September 14, 1995, and ends on the date of the transaction.

(b) Statutory categories of disqualified persons--(1) Family members. A person is a disqualified person with respect to any transaction with an applicable tax-exempt organization if the person is a member of the family of a person who is a disqualified person described in paragraph (a) of this section (other than as a result of this paragraph) with respect to any transaction with the same organization. For purposes of the following sentence, a legally adopted child of an individual is treated as a child of such individual by blood. A person's family is limited to --

(i) Spouse;

(ii) Brothers or sisters (by whole or half blood);

(iii) Spouses of brothers or sisters (by whole or half blood);

(iv) Ancestors;

(v) Children;

(vi) Grandchildren;

(vii) Great grandchildren; and

(viii) Spouses of children, grandchildren, and great grandchildren.

(2) Thirty-five percent controlled entities--(i) In general. A person is a disqualified person with respect to any transaction with an applicable tax-exempt organization if the person is a 35-percent controlled entity. A 35-percent controlled entity is--

(A) A corporation in which persons described in this section (except in paragraphs (b)(2) and (d) of this section) own more than 35 percent of the combined voting power;

(B) A partnership in which persons described in this section (except in paragraphs (b)(2) and (d) of this section) own more than 35 percent of the profits interest; or

(C) A trust or estate in which persons described in this section (except in paragraphs (b)(2) and (d) of this section) own more than 35 percent of the beneficial interest.

(ii) **Combined voting power.** For purposes of this paragraph (b)(2), combined voting power includes voting power represented by holdings of voting stock, direct or indirect, but does not include voting rights held only as a director, trustee, or other fiduciary.

(iii) **Constructive ownership rules--(A) Stockholdings.** For purposes of section 4958(f)(3) and this paragraph (b)(2), indirect stockholdings are taken into account as under section 267(c), except that in applying section 267(c)(4), the family of an individual shall include the members of the family specified in section 4958(f)(4) and paragraph (b)(1) of this section.

(B) **Profits or beneficial interest.** For purposes of section 4958(f)(3) and this paragraph (b)(2), the ownership of profits or beneficial interests shall be determined in accordance with the rules for constructive ownership of stock provided in section 267(c) (other than section 267(c)(3)), except that in applying section 267(c)(4), the family of an individual shall include the members of the family specified in section 4958(f)(4) and paragraph (b)(1) of this section.

(c) **Persons having substantial influence.** A person who holds any of the following powers, responsibilities, or interests is in a position to exercise substantial influence over the affairs of an applicable tax-exempt organization:

(1) **Voting members of the governing body.** This category includes any individual serving on the governing body of the organization who is entitled to vote on any matter over which the governing body has authority.

(2) **Presidents, chief executive officers, or chief operating officers.** This category includes any person who, regardless of title, has ultimate responsibility for implementing the decisions of the governing body or for supervising the management, administration, or operation of the organization. A person who

serves as president, chief executive officer, or chief operating officer has this ultimate responsibility unless the person demonstrates otherwise. If this ultimate responsibility resides with two or more individuals (e.g., co-presidents), who may exercise such responsibility in concert or individually, then each individual is in a position to exercise substantial influence over the affairs of the organization.

(3) **Treasurers and chief financial officers.** This category includes any person who, regardless of title, has ultimate responsibility for managing the finances of the organization. A person who serves as treasurer or chief financial officer has this ultimate responsibility unless the person demonstrates otherwise. If this ultimate responsibility resides with two or more individuals who may exercise the responsibility in concert or individually, then each individual is in a position to exercise substantial influence over the affairs of the organization.

(4) **Persons with a material financial interest in a provider-sponsored organization.** For purposes of section 4958, if a hospital that participates in a provider-sponsored organization (as defined in section 1855(e) of the Social Security Act, 42 U.S.C. 1395w-25) is an applicable tax-exempt organization, then any person with a material financial interest (within the meaning of section 501(o)) in the provider-sponsored organization has substantial influence with respect to the hospital.

(d) **Persons deemed not to have substantial influence.** A person is deemed not to be in a position to exercise substantial influence over the affairs of an applicable tax-exempt organization if that person is described in one of the following categories:

(1) **Tax-exempt organizations described in section 501(c)(3).** This category includes any organization described in section 501(c)(3) and exempt from tax under section 501(a).

(2) **Certain section 501(c)(4) organizations.** Only with respect to an applicable tax-exempt organization described in section 501(c)(4) and section 53.4958-2T(a)(3), this category includes any other organization so described.

(3) **Employees receiving economic benefits of less than a specified amount in a taxable year.** This category includes, for the taxable year in which benefits are provided, any full- or part-time employee of the applicable tax-exempt organization who--

(i) Receives economic benefits, directly or indirectly from the organization, of less than the amount referenced for a highly compensated employee in section 414(q)(1)(B)(i);

(ii) Is not described in section 53.4958-3T(b) or (c) with respect to the organization; and

(iii) Is not a substantial contributor to the organization within the meaning of section 507(d)(2)(A), taking into account only contributions received by the organization during its current taxable year and the four preceding taxable years.

(e) Facts and circumstances govern in all other cases--(1) In general. Whether a person who is not described in paragraph (b), (c) or (d) of this section is a disqualified person depends upon all relevant facts and circumstances.

(2) Facts and circumstances tending to show substantial influence. Facts and circumstances tending to show that a person has substantial influence over the affairs of an organization include, but are not limited to, the following--

(i) The person founded the organization;

(ii) The person is a substantial contributor to the organization (within the meaning of section 507(d)(2)(A)), taking into account only contributions received by the organization during its current taxable year and the four preceding taxable years;

(iii) The person's compensation is primarily based on revenues derived from activities of the organization that the person controls;

(iv) The person has or shares authority to control or determine a substantial portion of the organization's capital expenditures, operating budget, or compensation for employees;

(v) The person manages a discrete segment or activity of the organization that represents a substantial portion of the activities, assets, income, or expenses of the organization, as compared to the organization as a whole;

(vi) The person owns a controlling interest (measured by either vote or value) in a corporation, partnership, or trust that is a disqualified person; or

(vii) The person is a non-stock organization controlled, directly or indirectly, by one or more disqualified persons.

(3) Facts and circumstances tending to show no substantial influence. Facts and circumstances tending to show that a person does not have substantial influence over the affairs of an organization include, but are not limited to, the following --

(i) The person has taken a bona fide vow of poverty as an employee, agent, or on behalf, of a religious organization;

(ii) The person is an independent contractor (such as an attorney, accountant, or investment manager or advisor) whose sole relationship to the organization is providing professional advice (without having decision-making authority) with respect to transactions from which the independent contractor will not economically benefit either directly or indirectly (aside from customary fees received for the professional advice rendered);

(iii) The direct supervisor of the individual is not a disqualified person;

(iv) The person does not participate in any management decisions affecting the organization as a whole or a discrete segment or activity of the organization that represents a substantial portion of the activities, assets, income, or expenses of the organization, as compared to the organization as a whole; or
(v) Any preferential treatment a person receives based on the size of that person's donation is also offered to all other donors making a comparable contribution as part of a solicitation intended to attract a substantial number of contributions.

(f) Affiliated organizations. In the case of multiple organizations affiliated by common control or governing documents, the determination of whether a person does or does not have substantial influence shall be made separately for each applicable tax-exempt organization. A person may be a disqualified person with respect to transactions with more than one applicable tax-exempt organization.

(g) Examples. The following examples illustrate the principles of this section. Finding a person to be a disqualified person in the following examples does not indicate that an excess benefit transaction has occurred. If a person is a disqualified person, the rules of section 4958(c) and section 53.4958-4T apply to determine whether an excess benefit transaction has occurred. The examples are as follows:

Example 1. N, an artist by profession, works part-time at R, a local museum. In the first taxable year in which R employs N, R pays N a salary and provides no additional benefits to N except for free admission to the museum, a benefit R provides to all of its employees and volunteers. The total economic benefits N receives from R during the taxable year are less than the amount referenced for a highly compensated employee in section 414(q)(1)(B)(i). The part-time job constitutes N's only relationship with R. N is not related to any other disqualified person with respect to R. N is deemed not to be in a position to exercise substantial influence over the affairs of R. Therefore, N is not a disqualified person with respect to R in that year.

Example 2. The facts are the same as in Example 1, except that in addition to the salary that R pays N for N's services during the taxable year, R also purchases one of N's paintings for $x. The total of N's salary plus $x exceeds the amount referenced for highly compensated employees in section 414(q)(1)(B)(i). Consequently, whether N is in a position to exercise substantial influence over the affairs of R for that taxable year depends upon all of the relevant facts and circumstances.

Example 3: Q is a member of K, a section 501(c)(3) organization with a broad-based public membership. Members of K are entitled to vote only with respect to the annual election of directors and the approval of major organizational transactions such as a merger or dissolution. Q is not related to any other disqualified person of K. Q has no other relationship to K besides being a member of K and occasionally making modest donations to K. Whether Q is a disqualified person is determined by all relevant facts and circumstances. Q's voting rights, which are the same as granted to all members of K, do not place Q in a position to exercise substantial influence over K. Under these facts and circumstances, Q is not a disqualified person with respect K.

Example 4. E is the headmaster of Z, a school that is an applicable tax-exempt organization for purposes of section 4958. E reports to Z's board of trustees and has ultimate responsibility for supervising Z's day-to-day operations. For example, E can hire faculty members and staff, make changes to the school's curriculum and discipline students without specific board approval. Because E has ultimate responsibility for supervising the operation of Z, E is in a position to exercise substantial influence over the affairs of Z. Therefore, E is a disqualified person with respect to Z.

Example 5. Y is an applicable tax-exempt organization for purposes of section 4958 that decides to use bingo games as a method of generating revenue. Y enters into a contract with B, a company that operates bingo games. Under the contract, B manages the promotion and operation of the bingo activity, provides all necessary staff, equipment, and services, and pays Y q percent of the revenue from this activity. B retains the balance of the proceeds. Y provides no goods or services in connection with the bingo operation other than the use of its hall for the bingo games. The annual gross revenue earned from the bingo games represents more than half of Y's total annual revenue. B's compensation is primarily based on revenues from an activity B controls. B also manages a discrete activity of Y that represents a substantial portion of Y's income compared to the organization as a whole. Under these facts and circumstances, B is in a position to exercise substantial influence over the affairs of Y. Therefore, B is a disqualified person with respect to Y.

Example 6. The facts are the same as in Example 5, with the additional fact that P owns a majority of the stock of B and is actively involved in managing B. Because P owns a controlling interest (measured by either vote or value) in and actively manages B, P is also in a position to exercise substantial influence over the affairs of Y. Therefore, under these facts and circumstances, P is a disqualified person with respect to Y.

Example 7. A, an applicable tax-exempt organization for purposes of section 4958, owns and operates one acute care hospital. B, a for-profit corporation, owns and operates a number of hospitals. A and B form C, a limited liability company. In exchange for proportional ownership interests, A contributes its hospital, and B contributes other assets, to C. All of A's assets then consist of its membership interest in C. A continues to be operated for exempt purposes based almost exclusively on the activities it conducts through C. C enters into a management agreement with a management company, M, to provide day to day management services to C. M is generally subject to supervision by C's board, but

M is given broad discretion to manage C's day to day operation. Under these facts and circumstances, M is in a position to exercise substantial influence over the affairs of A because it has day to day control over the hospital operated by C, A's ownership interest in C is its primary asset, and C's activities form the basis for A's continued exemption as an organization described in section 501(c)(3). Therefore, M is a disqualified person with respect to A.

Example 8. T is a large university and an applicable tax-exempt organization for purposes of section 4958. L is the dean of the College of Law of T, a substantial source of revenue for T, including contributions from alumni and foundations. L is not related to any other disqualified person of T. L does not serve on T's governing body or have ultimate responsibility for managing the university as whole. However, as dean of the College of Law, L plays a key role in faculty hiring and determines a substantial portion of the capital expenditures and operating budget of the College of Law. L's compensation is greater than the amount referenced for a highly compensated employee in section 414(q)(1)(B)(i) in the year benefits are provided. L's management of a discrete segment of T that represents a substantial portion of the income of T (as compared to T as a whole) places L in a position to exercise substantial influence over the affairs of T. Under these facts and circumstances L is a disqualified person with respect to T.

Example 9. S chairs a small academic department in the College of Arts and Sciences of the same university T described in Example 8. S is not related to any other disqualified person of T. S does not serve on T's governing body or as an officer of T. As department chair, S supervises faculty in the department, approves the course curriculum, and oversees the operating budget for the department. S's compensation is greater than the amount referenced for a highly compensated employee in section 414(q)(1)(B)(i) in the year benefits are provided. Even though S manages the department, that department does not represent a substantial portion of T's activities, assets, income, expenses, or operating budget. Therefore, S does not participate in any management decisions affecting either T as a whole, or a discrete segment or activity of T that represents a substantial portion of its activities, assets, income, or expenses. Under these facts and circumstances, S does not have substantial influence over the affairs of T, and therefore S is not a disqualified person with respect to T.

Example 10. U is a large acute-care hospital that is an applicable tax-exempt organization for purposes of section 4958. U employs X as a radiologist. X gives instructions to staff with respect to the radiology work X conducts, but X does not supervise other U employees or manage any substantial part of U's operations. X's compensation is primarily in the form of a fixed salary. In addition, X is eligible to receive an incentive award based on revenues of the radiology department. X's compensation is greater than the amount referenced for a highly compensated employee in section 414(q)(1)(B)(i) in the year benefits are provided. X is not related to any other disqualified person of U. X does not serve on U's governing body or as an officer of U. Although U participates in a provider-sponsored organization (as defined in section 1855(e) of the Social Security Act), X does not have a material financial interest in that organization. X does not receive compensation primarily based on revenues derived from activities of U that X controls. X does not participate in any management decisions affecting either U as a whole or a discrete segment of U that represents a substantial portion of its activities, assets, income, or expenses. Under these facts and circumstances, X does not have substantial influence over the affairs of U, and therefore X is not a disqualified person with respect to U.

Example 11. W is a cardiologist and head of the cardiology department of the same hospital U described in Example 10. The cardiology department is a major source of patients admitted to U and consequently represents a substantial portion of U's income, as compared to U as a whole. W does not serve on U's governing board or as an officer of U. W does not have a material financial interest in the provider-sponsored organization (as defined in section 1855(e) of the Social Security Act) in which U participates. W receives a salary and retirement and welfare benefits fixed by a three-year renewable employment contract with U. W's compensation is greater than the amount referenced for a highly compensated employee in section 414(q)(1)(B)(i) in the year benefits are provided. As department head, W manages the cardiology department and has authority to allocate the budget for that department, which includes authority to distribute incentive bonuses among cardiologists according to criteria that W has authority to set. W's management of a discrete segment of U that represents a substantial portion of its income and activities (as compared to U as a whole) places W in a position to exercise substantial influence over the affairs of U. Under these facts and circumstances, W is a disqualified person with respect to U.

Example 12. M is a museum that is an applicable tax-exempt organization for purposes of section 4958. D provides accounting services and tax advice to M as an independent contractor in return for a fee. D has no other relationship with M and is not related to any disqualified person of M. D does not provide professional advice with respect to any transaction from which D might economically benefit either directly or indirectly (aside from fees received for the professional advice rendered). Because D's sole relationship to M is providing professional advice (without having decision-making authority) with respect to transactions from which D will not economically benefit either directly or indirectly (aside from customary fees received for the professional advice rendered), under these facts and circumstances, D is not a disqualified person with respect to M.

Example 13. F is a repertory theater company that is an applicable tax-exempt organization for purposes of section 4958. F holds a fund-raising campaign to pay for the construction of a new theater. J is a regular subscriber to F's productions who has made modest gifts to F in the past. J has no relationship to F other than as a subscriber and contributor. F solicits contributions as part of a broad public campaign intended to attract a large number of donors, including a substantial number of donors making large gifts. In its solicitations for contributions, F promises to invite all contributors giving $z or more to a special opening production and party held at the new theater. These contributors are also given a special number to call in F's office to reserve tickets for performances, make ticket exchanges, and make other special arrangements for their convenience. J makes a contribution of $z to F, which makes J a substantial contributor within the meaning of section 507(d)(2)(A), taking into account only contributions received by F during its current and the four preceding taxable years. J receives the benefits described in F's solicitation. Because F offers the same benefit to all donors of $z or more, the preferential treatment that J receives does not indicate that J is in a position to exercise substantial influence over the affairs of the organization. Therefore, under these facts and circumstances, J is not a disqualified person with respect to F.

Temp. Reg. § 53.4958-4T. Excess benefit transaction

(a) **Definition of excess benefit transaction--(1) In general.** An excess benefit transaction means any transaction in which an economic benefit is provided by an applicable tax-exempt organization directly or indirectly to or for the use of any disqualified person, and the value of the economic benefit provided exceeds the value of the consideration (including the performance of services) received for providing the benefit. Subject to the limitations of paragraph (c) of this section (relating to the treatment of economic benefits as compensation for the performance of services), to determine whether an excess benefit transaction has occurred, all consideration and benefits (except disregarded benefits described in paragraph (a)(4) of this section) exchanged between a disqualified person and the applicable tax-exempt organization and all entities the organization controls (within the meaning of paragraph (a)(2)(ii)(B) of this section) are taken into account. For example, in determining the reasonableness of compensation that is paid (or vests, or is no longer subject to a substantial risk of forfeiture) in one year, services performed in prior years may be taken into account. For rules regarding valuation standards, see paragraph (b) of this section. For the requirement that an applicable tax-exempt organization clearly indicate its intent to treat a benefit as compensation for services when paid, see paragraph (c) of this section.

(2) **Economic benefit provided indirectly--(i) In general.** A transaction that would be an excess benefit transaction if the applicable tax-exempt organization engaged in it directly with a disqualified person is likewise an excess benefit transaction when it is accomplished indirectly. An applicable tax-exempt organization may provide an excess benefit indirectly to a disqualified person through a controlled entity or through an intermediary, as described in paragraphs (a)(2)(ii) and (iii) of this section, respectively.

(ii) **Through a controlled entity--(A) In general.** An applicable tax-exempt organization may provide an excess benefit indirectly through the use of one or more entities it controls. For purposes of section 4958, economic benefits provided by a controlled entity will be treated as provided by the applicable tax-exempt organization.

(B) **Definition of control--(1) In general.** For purposes of this paragraph, control by an applicable tax-exempt organization means --

(i)   In the case of a stock corporation, ownership (by vote or value) of more than 50 percent of the stock in such corporation;

(ii)   In the case of a partnership, ownership of more than 50 percent of the profits interests or capital interests in the partnership;

(iii)   In the case of a nonstock organization (i.e., an entity in which no person holds a proprietary interest), that at least 50 percent of the directors or trustees of the organization are either representatives (including trustees, directors, agents, or employees) of, or directly or indirectly controlled by, an applicable tax-exempt organization; or

(iv)   In the case of any other entity, ownership of more than 50 percent of the beneficial interest in the entity.

(2) Constructive ownership. Section 318 (relating to constructive ownership of stock) shall apply for purposes of determining ownership of stock in a corporation. Similar principles shall apply for purposes of determining ownership of interests in any other entity.

(iii) Through an intermediary. An applicable tax-exempt organization may provide an excess benefit indirectly through an intermediary. An intermediary is any person (including an individual or a taxable or tax-exempt entity) who participates in a transaction with one or more disqualified persons of an applicable tax-exempt organization. For purposes of section 4958, economic benefits provided by an intermediary will be treated as provided by the applicable tax-exempt organization when --

(A)   An applicable tax-exempt organization provides an economic benefit to an intermediary; and

(B)   In connection with the receipt of the benefit by the intermediary--

(1)   There is evidence of an oral or written agreement or understanding that the intermediary will provide economic benefits to or for the use of a disqualified person; or

(2)   The intermediary provides economic benefits to or for the use of a disqualified person without a significant business purpose or exempt purpose of its own.

(iv) Examples. The following examples illustrate when economic benefits are provided indirectly under the rules of paragraph (a)(2) of this section:

Example 1. K is an applicable tax-exempt organization for purposes of section 4958. L is an entity controlled by K within the meaning of paragraph (a)(2)(ii)(B) of this section. J is employed by K, and is a disqualified person with respect to K. K pays J an annual salary of $12m, and reports that amount as compensation during calendar year 2001. Although J only performed services for K for nine months of 2001, J performed equivalent services for L during the remaining three months of 2001. Taking into account all of the economic benefits K provided to J, and all of the services J performed for K and L, $12m does not exceed the fair market value of the services J performed for K and L during 2001.

Therefore, under these facts, K does not provide an excess benefit to J directly or indirectly.

Example 2. F is an applicable tax-exempt organization for purposes of section 4958. D is an entity controlled by F within the meaning of paragraph (a)(2)(ii)(B) of this section. T is the chief executive officer (CEO) of F. As CEO, T is responsible for overseeing the activities of F. T's duties as CEO make him a disqualified person with respect to F. T's compensation package with F represents the maximum reasonable compensation for T's services as CEO. Thus, any additional economic benefits that F provides to T without T providing additional consideration constitute an excess benefit. D contracts with T to provide enumerated "consulting services" to D. However, the contract does not require T to perform any additional services for D that T is not already obligated to perform as F's chief executive officer. Therefore, any payment to T pursuant to the consulting contract with D represents an indirect excess benefit that F provides through a controlled entity, even if F, D, or T treats the additional payment to T as compensation.

Example 3. P is an applicable tax-exempt organization for purposes of section 4958. S is a taxable entity controlled by P within the meaning of paragraph (a)(2)(ii)(B) of this section. V is the chief executive officer of S, for which S pays V $w in salary and benefits. V also serves as a voting member of P's governing body. Consequently, V is a disqualified person with respect to P. P provides V with $x representing compensation for the services V provides P as a member of its governing body. Although $x represents reasonable compensation for the services V provides directly to P as a member of its governing body, the total compensation of $w + $x exceeds reasonable compensation for the services V provides to P and S collectively. Therefore, the portion of total compensation that exceeds reasonable compensation is an excess benefit provided to V.

Example 4. G is an applicable tax-exempt organization for section 4958 purposes. F is a disqualified person who was last employed by G in a position of substantial influence three years ago. H is an entity engaged in scientific research and is unrelated to either F or G. G makes a grant to H to fund a research position. H subsequently advertises for qualified candidates for the research position. F is among several highly qualified candidates who apply for the research position. H hires F. There was no evidence of an oral or written agreement or understanding with G that H will use G's grant to provide economic benefits to or for the use of F. Although G provided economic benefits to H, and in connection with the receipt of such benefits, H will provide economic benefits to or for the use of F, H acted with a significant business purpose or exempt purpose of its own. Under these facts, G did not provide an economic benefit to F indirectly through the use of an intermediary.

(3) Exception for fixed payments made pursuant to an initial contract--(i) In general. Except as provided in paragraph (iv), section 4958 does not apply to any fixed payment made to a person pursuant to an initial contract.

(ii) Fixed payment--(A) In general. For purposes of paragraph (a)(3)(i) of this section, fixed payment means an amount of cash or other property specified in the contract, or determined by a fixed formula specified in the contract, which is to be paid or transferred in exchange for the provision of specified services or property. A fixed formula may incorporate an amount that depends upon future specified events or contingencies, provided that no person exercises discretion when calculating the amount of a payment or deciding whether to make a payment (such as a bonus). A specified event or contingency may include the amount of revenues generated by (or other objective measure of) one or more activities of the applicable tax- exempt organization. A fixed payment does not include any amount paid to a person under a reimbursement (or similar) arrangement where discretion is exercised by any person with respect to the amount of expenses incurred or reimbursed.

(B) Special rules. Amounts payable pursuant to a qualified pension, profit-sharing, or stock bonus plan under Internal Revenue Code section 401(a), or pursuant to an employee benefit program that is subject to and satisfies coverage and nondiscrimination rules under the Code (e.g., sections 127 and 137), other than nondiscrimination rules under section 9802, are treated as fixed payments for purposes of this section, regardless of the applicable tax-exempt organization's discretion with respect to the plan or program. The fact that a person contracting with an applicable tax- exempt organization is expressly granted the choice whether to accept or reject any economic benefit is disregarded in determining whether the benefit constitutes a fixed payment for purposes of this paragraph.

(iii) Initial contract. For purposes of paragraph (a)(3)(i) of this section, initial contract means a binding written contract between an applicable tax-exempt organization and a person who was not a disqualified person within the meaning of section 4958(f)(1) and section 53.4958-3T immediately prior to entering into the contract.

(iv) Substantial performance required. Paragraph (a)(3)(i) of this section does not apply to any fixed payment made pursuant to the initial contract during any taxable year of the person contracting with the applicable tax-exempt organization if the person fails to perform substantially the person's obligations under the initial contract during that year.

(v) Treatment as a new contract. A written binding contract that provides that the contract is terminable or subject to cancellation by the applicable tax-exempt organization (other than as a result of a lack of substantial performance by the disqualified person, as described in paragraph (a)(3)(iv) of this section) without the other party's consent and without substantial penalty to the organization is treated as a new contract as of the earliest date that any such termination or cancellation, if made, would be effective. Additionally, if the parties make a material change to a contract, it is treated as a new contract as of the date the material change is effective. A material change includes an extension or renewal of the contract (other than an extension or renewal that results from the person contracting with the applicable tax-exempt organization unilaterally exercising an option expressly granted by the contract), or a more than incidental change to any amount payable under the contract. The new contract is tested under paragraph (a)(3)(iii) of this section to determine whether it is an initial contract for purposes of this section.

(vi) Evaluation of non-fixed payments. Any payment that is not a fixed payment (within the meaning of paragraph (a)(3)(ii) of this section) is evaluated to determine whether it constitutes an excess benefit transaction under section 4958. In making this determination, all payments and consideration exchanged between the parties are taken into account, including any fixed payments made pursuant to an initial contract with respect to which section 4958 does not apply.

(vii) Examples. The following examples illustrate the rules governing fixed payments made pursuant to an initial contract. Unless otherwise stated, assume that the person contracting with the applicable tax-exempt organization has performed substantially the person's obligations under the contract with respect to the payment. The examples are as follows:

Example 1. T is an applicable tax-exempt organization for purposes of section 4958. On January 1, 2000, T hires S as its chief financial officer by entering into a five-year written employment contract with S. S was not a disqualified person within the meaning of section 4958(f)(1) and section 53.4958-3T immediately prior to entering into the January 1, 2000, contract (initial contract). S's duties and responsibilities under the contract make S a disqualified person with respect to T (see section 53.4958-3T(c)(3)). Under the initial contract, T agrees to pay S an annual salary of $200,000, payable in monthly installments. The contract provides that, beginning in 2001, S's annual salary will be adjusted by the increase in the Consumer Price Index (CPI) for the prior year. Section 4958 does not apply because S's compensation under the contract is a fixed payment pursuant to an initial contract within the meaning of paragraph (a)(3) of this section. Thus, for section 4958 purposes, it is unnecessary to evaluate whether any portion of the compensation paid to S pursuant to the initial contract is an excess benefit transaction.

Example 2. The facts are the same as in Example 1, except that the initial contract provides that, in addition to a base salary of $200,000, T may pay S an annual performance-based bonus. The contract provides that T's governing body will determine the amount of the annual bonus as of the end of each year during the term of the contract, based on the board's evaluation of S's performance, but the bonus cannot exceed $100,000 per year. Unlike the base salary portion of S's compensation, the bonus portion of S's compensation is not a fixed payment pursuant to an initial contract, because the governing body has discretion over the amount, if any, of the bonus payment. Section 4958 does not apply to payment of the $200,000 base salary (as adjusted for inflation), because it is a fixed payment pursuant to an initial contract within the meaning of paragraph (a)(3) of this section. By contrast, the annual bonuses that may be paid to S under the initial contract are not protected by the initial contract exception. Therefore, each bonus payment will be evaluated under section 4958, taking into account all payments and consideration exchanged between the parties.

Example 3. The facts are the same as in Example 1, except that in 2001, T changes its payroll system, such that T makes biweekly, rather than monthly, salary payments to its employees. Beginning in 2001, T also grants its employees an additional two days of paid vacation each year. Neither change is a material change to S's initial contract within the meaning of paragraph (a)(3)(v) of this section. Therefore, section 4958 does not apply to the base salary payments to S due to the initial contract exception.

Example 4. The facts are the same as in Example 1, except that on January 1, 2001, S becomes the chief executive officer of T and a new chief financial officer is hired. At the same time, T's board of directors approves an increase in S's annual base salary from $200,000 to $240,000, effective on that day. These changes in S's employment relationship constitute material changes of the initial contract within the meaning of paragraph (a)(3)(v) of this section. As a result, S is treated as entering into a new contract with T on January 1, 2001, at which time S is a disqualified person within the meaning of section 4958(f)(1) and section 53.4958-3T. T's payments to S made pursuant to the new contract will be evaluated under section 4958, taking into account all payments and consideration exchanged between the parties.

Example 5. J is a performing arts organization and an applicable tax-exempt organization for purposes of section 4958. J hires W to become the chief executive officer of J. W was not a disqualified person within the meaning of section 4958(f)(1) and section 53.4958- 3T immediately prior to entering into the employment contract with J. As a result of this employment contract, W's duties and responsibilities make W a disqualified person with respect to J (see section 53.4958-3T(c)(2)). Under the contract, J will pay W $x (a specified amount) plus a bonus equal to 2 percent of the total season subscription sales that exceed $100z. The $x base salary is a fixed payment pursuant to an initial contract within the meaning of paragraph (a)(3) of this section. The bonus payment is also a fixed payment pursuant to an initial contract within the meaning of paragraph (a)(3) of this section, because no person exercises discretion when calculating the amount of the bonus payment or deciding whether the bonus will be paid. Therefore, section 4958 does not apply to any of J's payments to W pursuant to the employment contract due to the initial contract exception.

Example 6. Hospital B is an applicable tax-exempt organization for purposes of section 4958. Hospital B hires E as its chief operating officer. E was not a disqualified person within the meaning of section 4958(f)(1) and section 53.4958-3T immediately prior to entering into the employment contract with Hospital B. As a result of this employment contract, E's duties and responsibilities make E a disqualified person with respect to Hospital B (see section 53.4958- 3T(c)(2)). E's initial employment contract provides that E will have authority to enter into hospital management arrangements on behalf of Hospital B. In E's personal capacity, E owns more than 35 percent of the combined voting power of Company X. Consequently, at the time E becomes a disqualified person with respect to Hospital B, Company X also becomes a disqualified person with respect to Hospital B (see section 53.4958-3T(b)(2)(A)). E, acting on behalf of Hospital B as chief operating officer, enters into a contract with Company X under which Company X will provide billing and collection services to Hospital B. The initial contract exception of paragraph (a)(3)(i) of this section does not apply to the billing and collection services contract, because at the time that this contractual arrangement was entered into, Company X was a disqualified person with respect to Hospital B. Although E's employment contract (which is an initial contract) authorizes E to enter into hospital management arrangements on behalf of Hospital B, the payments made to Company X are not made pursuant to E's employment contract, but rather are made by Hospital B pursuant to a separate contractual arrangement with Company X. Therefore, even if payments made to Company X under the billing and collection services contract are fixed payments (within the meaning of paragraph (a)(3)(ii) of this section), section 4958 nonetheless applies to payments made by Hospital B to Company X because the billing and collection services contract itself does not constitute an initial contract under paragraph (a)(3)(iii) of this section. Accordingly, all payments made to Company X under the billing and collection services contract will be evaluated under section 4958.

Example 7. Hospital C, an applicable tax-exempt organization, enters into a contract with Company Y, under which Company Y will provide a wide range of hospital management services to Hospital C. Upon entering into this contractual arrangement, Company Y becomes a disqualified person with respect to Hospital C. The contract provides that Hospital C will pay Company Y a management fee of x percent of adjusted gross revenue (i.e., gross revenue increased by the cost of charity care provided to indigents) annually for a five-year period. The management services contract specifies the cost accounting system and the standards for indigents to be used in calculating the cost of charity care. The cost accounting system objectively defines the direct and indirect costs of all health care goods and services provided as charity care. Because Company Y was not a disqualified person with respect to Hospital C immediately before entering into the management services contract, that contract is an initial contract within the meaning of paragraph (a)(3)(iii) of this section. The annual management fee paid to Company Y is determined by a fixed formula specified in the contract, and is therefore a fixed payment within the meaning of paragraph (a)(3)(ii) of this section. Accordingly, section 4958 does not apply to the annual management fee due to the initial contract exception.

Example 8. The facts are the same as in Example 7, except that the management services contract also provides that Hospital C will reimburse Company Y on a monthly basis for certain expenses incurred by Company Y that are attributable to management services provided to Hospital C (e.g., legal fees and travel expenses). These reimbursement payments that Hospital C makes to Company Y for the various expenses covered by the contract are not fixed payments within the meaning of paragraph (a)(3)(ii) of this section, because Company Y exercises discretion with respect to the amount of expenses incurred. Therefore, any reimbursement payments that Hospital C pays pursuant to the contract will be evaluated under section 4958.

Example 9. X, an applicable tax-exempt organization for purposes of section 4958, hires C to conduct scientific research. On January 1, 2000, C enters into a three-year written employment contract with X ("initial contract"). Under the terms of the contract, C is required to work full-time at X's laboratory for a fixed annual salary of $90,000. Immediately prior to entering into the employment contract, C was not a disqualified person within the meaning of section 4958(f)(1) and section 53.4958-3T, nor did C become a disqualified person pursuant to the initial contract. However, two years after joining X, C marries D, who is the child of X's president. As D's spouse, C is a disqualified person within the meaning of section 4958(f)(1) and section 53.4958-3T with respect to X. Nonetheless, section 4958 does not apply to X's salary payments to C due to the initial contract exception.

Example 10. The facts are the same as in Example 9, except that the initial contract included a below-market loan provision under which C has the unilateral right to borrow up to a specified dollar amount from X at a specified interest rate for a specified term. After C's marriage to D, C borrows money from X to purchase a home under the terms of the initial contract. Section 4958 does not apply to X's loan to C due to the initial contract exception.

Example 11. The facts are the same as in Example 9, except that after C's marriage to D, C works only sporadically at the laboratory, and performs no other services for X. Notwithstanding that C fails to perform substantially C's obligations under the initial contract, X does not exercise its right to terminate the initial contract for nonperformance and continues to pay full salary to C. Pursuant to paragraph (a)(3)(iv) of this section, the initial contract exception does not apply to any payments made pursuant to the initial contract during any taxable year of C in which C fails to perform substantially C's obligations under the initial contract.

(4) Certain economic benefits disregarded for purposes of section 4958. The following economic benefits are disregarded for purposes of section 4958:

(i) Nontaxable fringe benefits. An economic benefit that is excluded from income under section 132, except any liability insurance premium, payment, or reimbursement that must be taken into account under section 53.4958-4T(b)(1)(ii)(B)(2);

(ii) Certain economic benefits provided to a volunteer for the organization. An economic benefit provided to a volunteer for the organization if the benefit is provided to the general public in exchange for a membership fee or contribution of $75 or less per year;

(iii) Certain economic benefits provided to a member of, or donor to, the organization. An economic benefit provided to a member of an organization solely on account of the payment of a membership fee, or to a donor solely on account of a contribution deductible under section 170, if--

(A) Any non-disqualified person paying a membership fee or making a contribution above a specified amount to the organization is given the option of receiving substantially the same economic benefit; and

(B) The disqualified person and a significant number of non- disqualified persons make a payment or contribution of at least the specified amount;

(iv) Economic benefits provided to a charitable beneficiary.
An economic benefit provided to a person solely as a member of a charitable class that the applicable tax-exempt organization intends to benefit as part of the accomplishment of the organization's exempt purpose; and

(v) Certain economic benefits provided to a governmental unit. Any transfer of an economic benefit to or for the use of a governmental unit defined in section 170(c)(1), if the transfer is for exclusively public purposes.

(b) Valuation standards--(1) In general. This section provides rules for determining the value of economic benefits for purposes of section 4958.

(i) Fair market value of property. The value of property, including the right to use property, for purposes of section 4958 is the fair market value (i.e., the price at which property or the right to use property would change hands between a willing buyer and a willing seller, neither being under any compulsion to buy, sell or transfer property or the right to use property, and both having reasonable knowledge of relevant facts).

(ii) Reasonable compensation--(A) In general. The value of services is the amount that would ordinarily be paid for like services by like enterprises under like circumstances (i.e., reasonable compensation). Section 162 standards apply in determining reasonableness of compensation, taking into account the aggregate benefits (other than any benefits specifically disregarded under paragraph (a)(4) of this section) provided to a person and the rate at which any deferred compensation accrues. The fact that a bonus or revenue-sharing arrangement is subject to a cap is a relevant factor in determining the reasonableness of compensation. The fact that a State or local legislative or agency body or court has authorized or approved a particular compensation package paid to a disqualified person is not determinative of the reasonableness of compensation for purposes of section 4958.

(B) Items included in determining the value of compensation for purposes of determining reasonableness under section 4958.

Except for economic benefits that are disregarded for purposes of section 4958 under paragraph (a)(4) of this section, compensation for purposes of determining reasonableness under section 4958 includes all economic benefits provided by an applicable tax-exempt organization in exchange for the performance of services. These benefits include, but are not limited to--

(1) All forms of cash and noncash compensation, including salary, fees, bonuses, severance payments, and deferred and noncash compensation described in section 53.4958-1T(e)(2);

(2) Unless excludable from income as a de minimis fringe benefit pursuant to section 132(a)(4), the payment of liability insurance premiums for, or the payment or reimbursement by the organization of--

(i) Any penalty, tax, or expense of correction owed under section 4958;

(ii) Any expense not reasonably incurred by the person in connection with a civil judicial or civil administrative proceeding arising out of the person's performance of services on behalf of the applicable tax-exempt organization; or

(iii) Any expense resulting from an act or failure to act with respect to which the person has acted willfully and without reasonable cause; and

(3) All other compensatory benefits, whether or not included in gross income for income tax purposes, including payments to welfare benefit plans, such as plans providing medical, dental, life insurance, severance pay, and disability benefits, and both taxable and nontaxable fringe benefits (other than fringe benefits described in section 132), including expense allowances or reimbursements, and foregone interest on loans.

(C) Inclusion in compensation for reasonableness determination does not govern income tax treatment. The determination of whether any item listed in paragraph (b)(1)(ii)(B) of this section is included in the disqualified person's gross income for income tax purposes is made on the basis of the provisions of chapter 1 of Subtitle A of the Internal Revenue Code, without regard to whether the item is taken into account for purposes of determining reasonableness of compensation under section 4958.

(2) Timing of reasonableness determination--(i) In general. The facts and circumstances to be taken into consideration in determining reasonableness of a fixed payment (within the meaning of paragraph (a)(3)(ii) of this section) are those existing on the date the parties enter into the contract pursuant to which the payment is made. However, in the event of substantial non-performance, reasonableness is determined based on all facts and circumstances, up to and including circumstances as of the date of payment. In the case of a payment that is not a fixed payment under a contract, reasonableness is determined based on all facts and circumstances, up to and including circumstances as of the date of payment. In no event shall circumstances existing at the date when the payment is questioned be considered in making a determination of the reasonableness of the payment.

(ii) Treatment as a new contract. For purposes of paragraph (b)(2)(i) of this section, a written binding contract that provides that the contract is terminable or subject to cancellation by the applicable tax-exempt organization without the other party's consent and without substantial penalty to the organization is treated as a new contract as of the earliest date that any such termination or cancellation, if made, would be effective. Additionally, if the parties make a material change to a contract (within the meaning of paragraph (a)(3)(v) of this section), it is treated as a new contract as of the date the material change is effective.

(iii) Examples. The following examples illustrate the timing of the reasonableness determination under the rules of this paragraph (b)(2):

Example 1. G is an applicable tax-exempt organization for purposes of section 4958. H is an employee of G and a disqualified person with respect to G. H's new multi-year employment contract provides for payment of a salary and provision of specific benefits pursuant to a qualified pension plan under Internal Revenue Code section 401(a) and an accident and health plan that meets the requirements of section 105(h)(2). The contract provides that H's salary will be adjusted by the increase in the Consumer Price Index (CPI) for the prior year. The contributions G makes to the qualified pension plan are equal to the maximum amount G is permitted to contribute under the rules applicable to qualified plans. Under these facts, all items comprising H's total compensation are treated as fixed payments within the meaning of paragraph (a)(3)(ii) of this section. Therefore, the reasonableness of H's compensation is determined based on the circumstances existing at the time G and H enter into the employment contract.

Example 2. N is an applicable tax-exempt organization for purposes of section 4958. On January 2, N's governing body enters into a new one-year employment contract with K, its executive director, who is a disqualified person with respect to N. The contract provides that K will receive a specified amount of salary, contributions to a qualified pension plan under Internal Revenue Code section 401(a), and other benefits pursuant to a section 125 cafeteria plan. In addition, the contract provides that N's governing body may, in its discretion, declare a bonus to be paid to K at any time during the year covered by the contract. K's salary and other specified benefits constitute fixed payments within the meaning of paragraph (a)(3)(ii) of this section. Therefore, the reasonableness of those economic benefits is determined on the date when the contract was made. However, because the bonus payment is not a fixed payment within the meaning of paragraph (a)(3)(ii) of this section, the determination of whether any bonus awarded to N is reasonable must be made based on all facts and circumstances (including all payments and consideration exchanged between the parties), up to and including circumstances as of the date of payment of the bonus.

(c) Establishing intent to treat economic benefit as consideration for the performance of services--(1) In general. An economic benefit is not treated as consideration for the performance of services unless the organization providing the benefit clearly indicates its intent to treat the benefit as compensation when the benefit is paid. Except as provided in paragraph (c)(2) of this section, an applicable tax-exempt organization (or entity controlled by an applicable tax-exempt organization, within the meaning of paragraph (a)(2)(ii)(B) of this section) is treated as clearly indicating its intent to provide an economic benefit as compensation for services only if the organization provides written substantiation that is contemporaneous with the transfer of the economic benefit at issue. If an organization fails to provide this contemporaneous substantiation, any services provided by the disqualified person will not be treated as provided in consideration for the economic benefit for purposes of determining the reasonableness of the transaction.

(2) Nontaxable benefits. For purposes of section 4958(c)(1)(A) and this section, an applicable tax-exempt organization is not required to indicate its intent to provide an economic benefit as compensation for services if the economic benefit is excluded from the disqualified person's gross income for income tax purposes on the basis of the provisions of chapter 1 of Subtitle A of the Internal Revenue Code. Examples of these benefits include, but are not limited to, employer-provided health benefits and contributions to a qualified pension, profit-sharing, or stock bonus plan under Internal Revenue Code section 401(a), and benefits described in sections 127 and 137. However, except for economic benefits that are disregarded for purposes of section 4958 under paragraph (a)(4) of this section, all compensatory benefits (regardless of the federal income tax treatment) provided by an organization in exchange for the performance of services are taken into account in determining the reasonableness of a person's compensation for purposes of section 4958.

(3) Contemporaneous substantiation--(i) Reporting of benefit. An applicable tax-exempt organization provides contemporaneous written substantiation of its intent to provide an economic benefit as compensation if--

(A) The organization reports the economic benefit as compensation on an original Federal tax information return with respect to the payment (e.g., Form W-2 or 1099) or with respect to the organization (e.g., Form 990), or on an amended Federal tax information return filed prior to the commencement of an Internal Revenue Service examination of the applicable tax-exempt organization or the disqualified person for the taxable year in which the transaction occurred (as determined under section 53.4958-1T(e)); or

(B) The recipient disqualified person reports the benefit as income on the person's original Federal tax return (e.g., Form 1040), or on the person's amended Federal tax return filed prior to the commencement of an Internal Revenue Service examination described in paragraph (c)(3)(i)(A) of this section.

(ii) Other evidence of contemporaneous substantiation. In addition, other written contemporaneous evidence may be used to demonstrate that the appropriate decision-making body or an authorized officer approved a transfer as compensation for services in accordance with established procedures, including an approved written employment contract executed on or before the date of the transfer, or documentation satisfying the requirements of section 53.4958-6T(a)(3) indicating that an authorized body approved the transfer as compensation for services on or before the date of the transfer.

(iii) Failure to report due to reasonable cause. If an applicable tax-exempt organization's failure to report an economic benefit as required under the Internal

Revenue Code is due to reasonable cause (within the meaning section 301.6724-1 of this chapter), then the organization will be treated as having clearly indicated its intent to provide an economic benefit as compensation for services. To show that its failure to report an economic benefit that should have been reported on an information return was due to reasonable cause, an applicable tax-exempt organization must establish that there were significant mitigating factors with respect to its failure to report (as described in section 301.6724-1(b) of this chapter), or the failure arose from events beyond the organization's control (as described in section 301.6724-1(c) of this chapter), and that the organization acted in a responsible manner both before and after the failure occurred (as described in section 301.6724-1(d) of this chapter).

(4) Examples. The following examples illustrate the requirement that an organization contemporaneously substantiate its intent to provide an economic benefit as compensation for services, as defined in paragraph (c) of this section:

Example 1. G is an applicable tax-exempt organization for purposes of section 4958. G hires an individual contractor, P, who is also the child of a disqualified person of G, to design a computer program for it. G executes a contract with P for that purpose in accordance with G's established procedures, and pays P $1,000 during the year pursuant to the contract. Before January 31 of the next year, G reports the full amount paid to P under the contract on a Form 1099 filed with the Internal Revenue Service. G will be treated as providing contemporaneous written substantiation of its intent to provide the $1,000 paid to P as compensation for the services P performed under the contract by virtue of either the Form 1099 filed with the Internal Revenue Service reporting the amount, or by virtue of the written contract executed between G and P.

Example 2. G is an applicable tax-exempt organization for purposes of section 4958. D is the chief operating officer of G, and a disqualified person with respect to G. D receives a bonus at the end of the year. G's accounting department determines that the bonus is to be reported on D's Form W-2. Due to events beyond G's control, the bonus is not reflected on D's Form W-2. As a result, D fails to report the bonus on his individual income tax return. G acts to amend Forms W-2 affected as soon as G is made aware of the error during an Internal Revenue Service examination. G's failure to report the bonus on an information return issued to D arose from events beyond G's control, and G acted in a responsible manner both before and after the failure occurred. Thus, because G had reasonable cause (within the meaning section 301.6724-1 of this chapter) for failing to report D's bonus, G will be treated as providing contemporaneous written substantiation of its intent to provide the bonus as compensation for services when paid.

§ 53.4958-5T. Transaction in which the amount of the economic benefit is determined in whole or in part by the revenues of one or more activities of the organization [Reserved]

§ 53.4958-6T Rebuttable presumption that a transaction is not an excess benefit transaction (temporary).

(a) **In general.** Payments under a compensation arrangement are presumed to be reasonable, and a transfer of property, or the right to use property, is presumed to be at fair market value, if the following conditions are satisfied--

(1) The compensation arrangement or the terms of the property transfer are approved in advance by an authorized body of the applicable tax-exempt organization (or an entity controlled by the organization within the meaning of section 53.4958-4T(a)(2)(ii)(B)) composed entirely of individuals who do not have a conflict of interest (within the meaning of paragraph (c)(1)(iii) of this section) with respect to the compensation arrangement or property transfer, as described in paragraph (c)(1) of this section;

(2) The authorized body obtained and relied upon appropriate data as to comparability prior to making its determination, as described in paragraph (c)(2) of this section; and

(3) The authorized body adequately documented the basis for its determination concurrently with making that determination, as described in paragraph (c)(3) of this section.

(b) **Rebutting the presumption.** If the three requirements of paragraph (a) of this section are satisfied, then the Internal Revenue Service may rebut the presumption that arises under paragraph (a) of this section only if it develops sufficient contrary evidence to rebut the probative value of the comparability data relied upon by the authorized body. With respect to any fixed payment (within the meaning of section 53.4958-4T(a)(3)(ii)), rebuttal evidence is limited to evidence relating to facts and circumstances existing on the date the parties enter into the contract pursuant to which the payment is made (except in the event of substantial nonperformance). With respect to all other payments (including non-fixed payments subject to a cap, as described in paragraph (d)(2) of this section), rebuttal evidence may include facts and circumstances up to and including the date of payment. See section 53.4958-4T(b)(2)(i).

(c) **Requirements for invoking rebuttable presumption--(1) Approval by an authorized body --(i) In general.** An authorized body means--

(A) The governing body (i.e., the board of directors, board of trustees, or equivalent controlling body) of the organization;

(B) A committee of the governing body, which may be composed of any individuals permitted under State law to serve on such a committee, to the extent that the committee is permitted by State law to act on behalf of the governing body; or

(C) To the extent permitted under State law, other parties authorized by the governing body of the organization to act on its behalf by following procedures specified by the governing body in approving compensation arrangements or property transfers.

(ii) **Individuals not included on authorized body.** For purposes of determining whether the requirements of paragraph (a) of this section have been met with respect to a specific compensation arrangement or property transfer, an individual is not included on the authorized body when it is reviewing a transaction if that individual meets with other members only to answer questions, and otherwise recuses himself or herself from the meeting and is not present during debate and voting on the compensation arrangement or property transfer.

(iii) **Absence of conflict of interest.** A member of the authorized body does not have a conflict of interest with respect to a compensation arrangement or property transfer only if the member --

(A) Is not a disqualified person participating in or economically benefiting from the compensation arrangement or property transfer, and is not a member of the family of any such disqualified person, as described in section 4958(f)(4) or section 53.4958-3T(b)(1);

(B) Is not in an employment relationship subject to the direction or control of any disqualified person participating in or economically benefiting from the compensation arrangement or property transfer;

(C) Does not receive compensation or other payments subject to approval by any disqualified person participating in or economically benefiting from the compensation arrangement or property transfer;

(D) Has no material financial interest affected by the compensation arrangement or property transfer; and

(E) Does not approve a transaction providing economic benefits to any disqualified person participating in the compensation arrangement or property transfer, who in turn has approved or will approve a transaction providing economic benefits to the member.

(2) **Appropriate data as to comparability--(i) In general.** An authorized body has appropriate data as to comparability if, given the knowledge and expertise of its members, it has information sufficient to determine whether, under the standards set forth in section 53.4958-4T(b), the compensation arrangement in

its entirety is reasonable or the property transfer is at fair market value. In the case of compensation, relevant information includes, but is not limited to, compensation levels paid by similarly situated organizations, both taxable and tax-exempt, for functionally comparable positions; the availability of similar services in the geographic area of the applicable tax-exempt organization; current compensation surveys compiled by independent firms; and actual written offers from similar institutions competing for the services of the disqualified person. In the case of property, relevant information includes, but is not limited to, current independent appraisals of the value of all property to be transferred; and offers received as part of an open and competitive bidding process.

(ii) Special rule for compensation paid by small organizations. For organizations with annual gross receipts (including contributions) of less than $1 million reviewing compensation arrangements, the authorized body will be considered to have appropriate data as to comparability if it has data on compensation paid by three comparable organizations in the same or similar communities for similar services. No inference is intended with respect to whether circumstances falling outside this safe harbor will meet the requirement with respect to the collection of appropriate data.

(iii) Application of special rule for small organizations. For purposes of determining whether the special rule for small organizations described in paragraph (c)(2)(ii) of this section applies, an organization may calculate its annual gross receipts based on an average of its gross receipts during the three prior taxable years. If any applicable tax-exempt organization is controlled by or controls another entity (as defined in section 53.4958-4T(a)(2)(ii)(B)), the annual gross receipts of such organizations must be aggregated to determine applicability of the special rule stated in paragraph (c)(2)(ii) of this section.

(iv) Examples. The following examples illustrate the rules for appropriate data as to comparability for purposes of invoking the rebuttable presumption of reasonableness described in this section. In all examples, compensation refers to the aggregate value of all benefits provided in exchange for services. The examples are as follows:

Example 1. Z is a university that is an applicable tax-exempt organization for purposes of section 4958. Z is negotiating a new contract with Q, its president, because the old contract will expire at the end of the year. In setting Q's compensation for its president at $600x per annum, the executive committee of the Board of Trustees relies solely on a national survey of compensation for university presidents that indicates university presidents receive annual compensation in the range of $100x to $700x; this survey does not divide its data by any criteria, such as the number of students served by the institution, annual revenues, academic ranking, or geographic location. Although many members of the executive committee have significant business experience, none of the members has any particular expertise in higher education compensation matters. Given the failure of the survey to provide information specific to universities comparable to Z, and because no other information was presented, the executive committee's decision with respect to Q's compensation was not based upon appropriate data as to comparability.

Example 2. The facts are the same as in Example 1, except that the national compensation survey divides the data regarding compensation for university presidents into categories based on various university-specific factors, including the size of the institution (in terms of the number of students it serves and the amount of its revenues) and geographic area. The survey data shows that university presidents at institutions comparable to and in the same geographic area as Z receive annual compensation in the range of $200x to $300x. The executive committee of the Board of Trustees of Z relies on the survey data and its evaluation of Q's many years of service as a tenured professor and high-ranking university official at Z in setting Q's compensation at $275x annually. The data relied upon by the executive committee constitutes appropriate data as to comparability.

Example 3. X is a tax-exempt hospital that is an applicable tax- exempt organization for purposes of section 4958. Before renewing the contracts of X's chief executive officer and chief financial officer, X's governing board commissioned a customized compensation survey from an independent firm that specializes in consulting on issues related to executive placement and compensation. The survey covered executives with comparable responsibilities at a significant number of taxable and tax-exempt hospitals. The survey data are sorted by a number of different variables, including the size of the hospitals and the nature of the services they provide, the level of experience and specific responsibilities of the executives, and the composition of the annual compensation packages. The board members were provided with the survey results, a detailed written analysis comparing the hospital's executives to those covered by the survey, and an opportunity to ask questions of a member of the firm that prepared the survey. The survey, as prepared and presented to X's board, constitutes appropriate data as to comparability.

Example 4. The facts are the same as in Example 3, except that one year later, X is negotiating a new contract with its chief executive officer. The governing board of X has no information indicating that the relevant market conditions have changed or that the results of the prior year's survey are no longer valid. Therefore, X may continue to rely on the independent compensation survey prepared for the prior year in setting annual compensation under the new contract.

Example 5. W is a local repertory theater and an applicable tax- exempt organization for purposes of section 4958. W has had annual gross receipts ranging from $400,000 to $800,000 over its past three taxable years. In determining the next year's compensation for W's artistic director, the board of directors of W relies on data compiled from a telephone survey of three other unrelated repertory theaters of similar size in similar communities. A member of the board drafts a brief written summary of the annual compensation information obtained from this informal survey. The annual compensation information obtained in the telephone survey is appropriate data as to comparability.

(3) Documentation--(i) For a decision to be documented adequately, the written or electronic records of the authorized body must note--

(A) The terms of the transaction that was approved and the date it was approved;

(B) The members of the authorized body who were present during debate on the transaction that was approved and those who voted on

(C) The comparability data obtained and relied upon by the authorized body and how the data was obtained; and

(D) Any actions taken with respect to consideration of the transaction by anyone who is otherwise a member of the authorized body but who had a conflict of interest with respect to the transaction.

(ii) If the authorized body determines that reasonable compensation for a specific arrangement or fair market value in a specific property transfer is higher or lower than the range of comparability data obtained, the authorized body must record the basis for its determination. For a decision to be documented concurrently, records must be prepared before the later of the next meeting of the authorized body or 60 days after the final action or actions of the authorized body are taken. Records must be reviewed and approved by the authorized body as reasonable, accurate and complete within a reasonable time period thereafter.

(d) No presumption with respect to non-fixed payments until amounts are determined--(1) In general. Except as provided in paragraph (d)(2) of this section, in the case of a payment that is not a fixed payment (within the meaning of section 53.4958- 4T(a)(3)(ii)), the rebuttable presumption of this section arises only after the exact amount of the payment is determined, or a fixed formula for calculating the payment is specified, and the three requirements for the presumption under paragraph (a) of this section subsequently are satisfied. See section 53.4958-4T(b)(2)(i).

(2) Special rule for certain non-fixed payments subject to a cap. If the authorized body approves an employment contract with a disqualified person that includes a non-fixed payment (such as a discretionary bonus) subject to a specified cap, the authorized body may establish a rebuttable presumption with respect to the non-fixed payment at the time the employment contract is entered into if--

(i) Prior to approving the contract, the authorized body obtains appropriate comparability data indicating that a fixed payment of up to a certain amount to the particular disqualified person would represent reasonable compensation;

(ii) The maximum amount payable under the contract (taking into account both fixed and non-fixed payments) does not exceed the amount referred to in paragraph (d)(2)(i) of this section; and

(iii) The other requirements for the rebuttable presumption of reasonableness under paragraph (a) of this section are satisfied.

(e) **No inference from absence of presumption.** The fact that a transaction between an applicable tax-exempt organization and a disqualified person is not subject to the presumption described in this section neither creates any inference that the transaction is an excess benefit transaction, nor exempts or relieves any person from compliance with any federal or state law imposing any obligation, duty, responsibility, or other standard of conduct with respect to the operation or administration of any applicable tax-exempt organization.

(f) **Period of reliance on rebuttable presumption.** Except as provided in paragraph (d) of this section with respect to non-fixed payments, the rebuttable presumption applies to all payments made or transactions completed in accordance with a contract, provided that the provisions of paragraph (a) of this section were met at the time the parties entered into the contract.

Temp. Reg. § 53.4958-7T. Correction

(a) **In general.** An excess benefit transaction is corrected by undoing the excess benefit to the extent possible, and taking any additional measures necessary to place the applicable tax-exempt organization involved in the excess benefit transaction in a financial position not worse than that in which it would be if the disqualified person were dealing under the highest fiduciary standards. Paragraph (b) of this section describes the acceptable forms of correction. Paragraph (c) of this section defines the correction amount. Paragraph (d) of this section describes correction where a contract has been partially performed. Paragraph (e) of this section describes correction where the applicable tax-exempt organization involved in the transaction has ceased to exist or is no longer tax-exempt. Paragraph (f) of this section provides examples illustrating correction.

(b) **Form of correction--(1) Cash or cash equivalents.** Except as provided in paragraphs (b)(3) and (4) of this section, a disqualified person corrects an excess benefit only by making a payment in cash or cash equivalents, excluding payment by a promissory note, to the applicable tax-exempt organization equal to the correction amount, as defined in paragraph (c) of this section.

(2) **Anti-abuse rule.** A disqualified person will not satisfy the requirements of paragraph (b)(1) of this section if the Commissioner determines that the disqualified person engaged in one or more transactions with the applicable tax-exempt organization to circumvent the requirements of this correction section, and as a result, the disqualified person effectively transferred property other than cash or cash equivalents.

(3) Special rule relating to nonqualified deferred compensation. If an excess benefit transaction results, in whole or in part, from the vesting (as described in section 53.4958-1T(e)(2)) of benefits provided under a nonqualified deferred compensation plan, then, to the extent that such benefits have not yet been distributed to the disqualified person, the disqualified person may correct the portion of the excess benefit resulting from such undistributed deferred compensation by relinquishing any right to receive such benefits (including any earnings thereon).

(4) Return of specific property--(i) In general. A disqualified person may, with the agreement of the applicable tax- exempt organization, make a payment by returning specific property previously transferred in the excess benefit transaction. In this case, the disqualified person is treated as making a payment equal to the lesser of--

(A) The fair market value of the property determined on the date the property is returned to the organization; or

(B) The fair market value of the property on the date the excess benefit transaction occurred.

(ii) Payment not equal to correction amount. If the payment described in paragraph (b)(4)(i) of this section is less than the correction amount (as described in paragraph (c) of this section), the disqualified person must make an additional cash payment to the organization equal to the difference. Conversely, if the payment described in paragraph (b)(4)(i) of this section exceeds the correction amount (as described in paragraph (c) of this section), the organization may make a cash payment to the disqualified person equal to the difference.

(iii) Disqualified person may not participate in decision. Any disqualified person who received an excess benefit from the excess benefit transaction may not participate in the applicable tax-exempt organization's decision whether to accept the return of specific property under paragraph (b)(4)(i) of this section.

(c) Correction amount. The correction amount with respect to an excess benefit transaction equals the sum of the excess benefit (as defined in section 53.4958-1T(b)) and interest on the excess benefit. The amount of the interest charge for purposes of this section is determined by multiplying the excess benefit by an interest rate, compounded annually, for the period from the date the excess benefit transaction occurred (as defined in section 53.4958-1T(e)) to the date of correction. The interest rate used for this purpose must be a rate that equals or exceeds the applicable Federal rate (AFR), compounded annually, for the month in which the transaction occurred. The period from the date the excess benefit transaction occurred to the date of correction is used to determine whether the appropriate AFR is the Federal short-term rate, the Federal mid-term rate, or the Federal long-term rate. See section 1274(d)(1)(A).

(d) Correction where contract has been partially performed. If the excess benefit transaction arises under a contract that has been partially performed, termination of the contractual relationship between the organization and the disqualified person is not required in order to correct. However, the parties may need to modify the terms of any ongoing contract to avoid future excess benefit transactions.

(e) Correction in the case of an applicable tax-exempt organization that has ceased to exist, or is no longer tax-exempt--(1) In general. A disqualified person must correct an excess benefit transaction in accordance with this paragraph where the applicable tax-exempt organization that engaged in the transaction no longer exists or is no longer described in section 501(c)(3) or (4) and exempt from tax under section 501(a).

(2) Section 501(c)(3) organizations. In the case of an excess benefit transaction with a section 501(c)(3) applicable tax-exempt organization, the disqualified person must pay the correction amount, as defined in paragraph (c) of this section, to another organization described in section 501(c)(3) and exempt from tax under section 501(a) in accordance with the dissolution clause contained in the constitutive documents of the applicable tax-exempt organization involved in the excess benefit transaction, provided that the other organization is not related to the disqualified person.

(3) Section 501(c)(4) organizations. In the case of an excess benefit transaction with a section 501(c)(4) applicable tax-exempt organization, the disqualified person must pay the correction amount, as defined in paragraph (c) of this section, to a successor section 501(c)(4) organization or, if no tax-exempt successor, to any section 501(c)(3) or other section 501(c)(4) organization not related to the disqualified person.

(f) Examples. The following examples illustrate the principles of this section describing the requirements of correction:

Example 1. W is an applicable tax-exempt organization for purposes of section 4958. D is a disqualified person with respect to W. W employed D in 1999 and made payments totaling $12t to D as compensation throughout the taxable year. The fair market value of D's services in 1999 was $7t. Thus, D received excess compensation in the amount of $5t, the excess benefit for purposes of section 4958. In accordance with section 53.4958-1T(e)(1), the excess benefit transaction with respect to the series of compensatory payments during 1999 is deemed to occur on December 31, 1999, the last day of D's taxable year. In order to correct the excess benefit transaction on June 30, 2002, D must pay W, in cash or cash equivalents, excluding payment with a promissory note, $5t (the excess benefit) plus interest on $5t for the period from the date the excess benefit transaction occurred to the date of correction (i.e., December 31, 1999, to June 30, 2002). Because this period is not more than three years, the interest rate D must use to determine the interest on the excess benefit must equal or exceed the short-term AFR, compounded annually, for December, 1999 (5.74%, compounded annually).

Example 2. X is an applicable tax-exempt organization for purposes of section 4958. B is a disqualified person with respect to X. On January 1, 2000, B paid X $6v for Property F. Property F had a fair market value of $10v on January 1, 2000. Thus, the sales transaction on that date provided an excess benefit to B in the amount of $4v. In order to correct the excess benefit on July 5, 2005, B pays X, in cash or cash equivalents, excluding payment with a promissory note, $4v (the excess benefit) plus interest on $4v for the period from the date the excess benefit transaction occurred to the date of correction (i.e., January 1, 2000, to July 5, 2005). Because this period is over three but not over nine years, the interest rate B must use to determine the interest on the excess benefit must equal or exceed the mid-term AFR, compounded annually, for January, 2000 (6.21%, compounded annually).

Example 3. The facts are the same as in Example 2, except that B offers to return Property F. X agrees to accept the return of Property F, a decision in which B does not participate. Property F has declined in value since the date of the excess benefit transaction. On July 5, 2005, the property has a fair market value of $9v. For purposes of correction, B's return of Property F to X is treated as a payment of $9v, the fair market value of the property determined on the date the property is returned to the organization. If $9v is greater than the correction amount ($4v plus interest on $4v at a rate that equals or exceeds 6.21%, compounded annually, for the period from January 1, 2000, to July 5, 2005), then X may make a cash payment to B equal to the difference.

Example 4. The facts are the same as in Example 3, except that Property F has increased in value since January 1, 2000, the date the excess benefit transaction occurred, and on July 5, 2005, has a fair market value of $13v. For purposes of correction, B's return of Property F to X is treated as a payment of $10v, the fair market value of the property on the date the excess benefit transaction occurred. If $10v is greater than the correction amount ($4v plus interest on $4v at a rate that equals or exceeds 6.21%, compounded annually, for the period from January 1, 2000, to July 5, 2005), then X may make a cash payment to B equal to the difference.

Example 5. The facts are the same as in Example 2. Assume that the correction amount B paid X in cash on July 5, 2005, was $5.58v. On July 4, 2005, X loaned $5.58v to B, in exchange for a promissory note signed by B in the amount of $5.58v, payable with interest at a future date. These facts indicate that B engaged in the loan transaction to circumvent the requirement of this section that (except as provided in paragraph (b)(3) or (4) of this section), the correction amount must be paid only in cash or cash equivalents. As a result, the Commissioner may determine that B effectively transferred property other than cash or cash equivalents, and therefore did not satisfy the correction requirements of this section.

§ 53.4958-8T. Special rules

(a) **Substantive requirements for exemption still apply.** Section 4958 does not affect the substantive standards for tax exemption under section 501(c)(3) or (4), including the requirements that the organization be organized and operated exclusively for exempt purposes, and that no part of its net earnings inure to the benefit of any private shareholder or individual. Thus, regardless of whether a particular transaction is subject to excise taxes under section 4958, existing principles and rules may be implicated, such as the limitation on private benefit. For example, transactions that are not subject to section 4958 because of the initial contract exception described in section 53.4958-4T(a)(3) may, under certain circumstances, jeopardize the organization's tax-exempt status.

(b) **Interaction between section 4958 and section 7611 rules for church tax inquiries and examinations.** The procedures of section 7611 will be used in initiating and conducting any inquiry or examination into whether an excess benefit transaction has occurred between a church and a disqualified person. For purposes of this rule, the reasonable belief required to initiate a church tax inquiry is satisfied if there is a reasonable belief that a section 4958 tax is due from a disqualified person with respect to a transaction involving a church. See section 301.7611-1 Q&A 19 of this chapter.

(c) **Three year duration of these temporary regulations.** Sections 53.4958-1T through 53.4958-8T will cease to apply on January 9, 2004.